Steelhead
FLY TYING GUIDE

H. KENT HELVIE

COLOR FLY PLATES BY
MARK KIRCHNER

Frank
Amato
PORTLAND

DEDICATION

This book is dedicated to my wife Renee'
who stuck by me and pushed me and didn't leave me.

Frank Amato Publications Inc.
P.O. Box 82112
Portland, Oregon 97282
(503) 653-8108

Photo Credits:
Mark Kirchner: front cover, all fly plate photographs
and pages 6, 10, 17, 19 and 25
H. Kent Helvie: back cover, all instructional fly tying photographs
and pages 14, 20, 22, 26, 56, 80 and 88
Frank Amato: title page photograph and pages 8 and 12
Dec Hogan: 21

Book design and layout: Tony Amato

Softbound ISBN: 1-878175-85-8
Hardbound ISBN: 1-878175-86-6
Softbound UPC: 0-66066-00169-6
Hardbound UPC: 0-66066-00170-2

Printed in HONG KONG

10 9 8 7 6 5 4 3

TABLE OF
CONTENTS

Acknowledgments

WRITING YOUR FIRST BOOK IS FAR MORE overwhelming than one suspects at the beginning. What starts as a rough outline goes through many changes before the publication is ready to go to the printer. Often, as in my case, the book resembles the first draft very little. The time spent relegates the author to what seems like a less than minimum wage job. So the writing of a book like this becomes a labor which transcends more than monetary gain. This book is a reflection of much time and love for the art of fly tying.

At the time I began *Steelhead Fly Tying Guide*, my wife and I were expecting our son Caleb. As I watched my son grow, my outlook on things changed and so did my writing. What started as a quick job began to slow as my son needed and wanted more of my time. Often I would look down in mid-thought to hear Caleb say, "DaDa, slide?" I would be dragged away by my finger and end up spending hours playing with my son, time well spent. My dear wife, Renee', would try to let me work but fatherhood comes first. Consequently, the book went over schedule.

This is where my thanks to Frank Amato come in. During the latter part of my writing, Frank would call from time to time to check on my progress but I never felt pressured. We would discuss things about layout, photographs, numbers of flies and I always felt relaxed at the end of our talks. Thank you, Frank.

Others who deserve thanks are the many tiers who provided me with flies and information. Some helped direct me to other tiers who had things to offer. These key people include George Cook, Greg Scot Hunt, Brad Burden and Joe Rossano.

A special thanks goes to Joe Howell of the Blue Heron Fly Shop. Joe taught me much about tying although I never took a lesson from him. What Joe taught me was that the beauty of a fly goes far beyond the tiny head and should include the whole fly. Joe helped me learn to enjoy my own work and be satisfied with what pleased me. Joe is the ultimate fly tier, being very good at all aspects of the art. Thank you, Joe, for your time.

My father got me started at the tying bench at an early age. He taught me all he knew about flies and life. The life part is what was so important, the value of a person is not measured in what things they own but in the character they possess. His patience was great and he let me get into his stuff.

I first met Mark Kirchner over the phone. Over the few years that I have known him, he has shown me his talents as a fly tier and photographer. Many of his photographs inspired me to do better at my Atlantic salmon fly tying. He is a perfectionist and his work shows it. My thanks go out to him for gracing the pages of this book with his color plates and his flies.

My wife deserves the most credit though. While we were starting a family, she let me start a project that was all-consuming. She pushed me when needed and encouraged me often. Although this book became my mistress, Renee' never left me. She may have gotten jealous but she never left me. A good wife like her is a gem in a man's crown. The Lord gives you a wife like Renee'. Verbal thanks are too shallow. I owe you, dear.

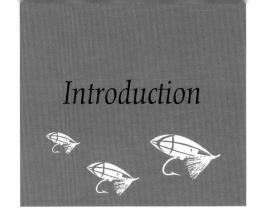

Introduction

OVER THE PAST DECADE THE INCREASE IN THE number of steelhead fly fishermen has been tremendous. Fly fishing has finally reached the position of respectability that it deserves. As the quality of tackle fishermen use has increased, so has the vast array of flies and the quality of the tiers increased.

During the Victorian age of Atlantic salmon angling in the United Kingdom the flies fishermen used were works of art and often seen as status symbols. Sirs, kings and dukes were the fishermen at that time and flies with names such as Baron Dawson, Sir Herbert and the Duke of Sutherland were often used. Many were so lavishly dressed that the local angler had to resort to 'lowly' hairwing patterns or hand-me-downs from the wealthy.

Today's steelhead fisherman has the choice of using some ornate and lovely steelhead flies that rival many of the classic salmon flies in beauty and the classic bucktail steelhead flies. To open a steelhead angler's fly box is to expose an artist's pallet of colors, hues and tones blended in feathers, furs and tinsels that trigger thoughts of sheer artistry and beauty.

Never before has a fly tier had so many options concerning materials, hooks and patterns. We have observed an information explosion over the last twenty years completely unknown to the outside world of deprived, nonfishermen.

Steelhead fly fishing and its flies no longher take a backseat to the Atlantic salmon angler. In previous generations steelhead anglers used hybrid flies that were quite often the result of a tier's inability to obtain materials required to tie a proper Jock Scott or Durham Ranger. The Kate, another early Atlantic salmon pattern, also resulted in many reduced and mutated versions. In the early days of steelheading the procurement of many materials was limited on the West coast. This led to an evolution of many of today's steelhead patterns.

If I had a dozen innovative tiers each construct a Green Butted Skunk I would receive twelve distinctly different flies. While the Green Butted Skunk is a good standard pattern it is just that, a pattern.

A tailor may use a pattern to make a suit but he might choose to use silk instead of wool or deem it necessary to alter the cut of the suit to fit the customer or the situation at hand. The pattern was used but only as a guide. He was innovative and responsive to his clients needs and was able to make a suit just right for the situation.

The same applies when tying a fly. By altering the choice of materials, chartreuse ostrich herl for the butt, black silk floss and seal dubbing for black chenille or Arctic fox for bucktail, the whole character of the fly is changed but you are still using the same pattern. Proportions and choice of materials are subject to change.

Over the years one sign of a well-tied fly was a small, neat head. Recently that small head has become a tiny dot of head cement covering just a few wraps of thread. Some tiers have tied flies without a head at all. Mark Kirchner of Newport Beach, California sent me a Peacock Spade Fly without a head, a very interesting fly.

The small head, in itself, does not constitute a well-tied fly. A fly tied to be fished with should be constructed to take some abuse without coming unraveled. While this may lead some people to believe that a fly cannot be constructed to be durable and also have a small head, this is not true. Through proper tying techniques a solid, well-built fly with a trim body and tiny head is possible.

I won't try to sell anyone on the idea that the only beautiful fly is one with an almost nonexistent head. Every tier develops a method and form they are happy with.

Joe Howell, owner of the Blue Heron Fly Shop in Idleyld Park, Oregon is well-known for his Spey flies and is an extremely accomplished tier whose style and method provides a nice clean head that is not tiny. Nonetheless, I feel Joe is one of the finest tiers in the Northwest. Just through conversation with Joe I have learned a lot about developing my own style and being happy with it.

Too often we concentrate on the head and not the whole fly. The proportions for the body, hackle and wing are also involved in the aesthetic value of a fly. While the actual size of the wing will vary from one tier to the next it should provide for a balanced fly.

Throughout this book I share various methods of my own, and other tier's, that will help you tie a well-balanced fly that is trim, without unwanted bulk. I show different ways to create a small head but keep in mind that a tiers style should be his or her own and you must find a balance that you are happy with and then maybe a tiny head won't be so critical to you.

1 History

IN THE EARLY DAYS OF STEELHEADING THE WEST was still a "wild" place to most of the rest of the country. Western writer, Zane Grey, wrote his amazing fishing and hunting stories for the "city folks" to admire and dream about. Times were rough, with most of the Northwest's steelhead rivers being a pack in trip of several days. The Rogue and North Umpqua left Grey's readers in awe with its tales of fish camps and huge fish that would tear most eastern limestone tackle to pieces. Zane Grey's stories were often bigger than life and so the roots of steelhead fly fishing were planted.

Yet the birth of steelheading began years before Mr. Grey hooked his first steelhead on the Rogue in 1922. To find the roots of steelheading one must travel back to the late 1800s and the Eel River. The Eel River was the hub for the first steelheaders, and the earliest steelhead patterns came out of northern California.

Tackle was available through local shops and some was even manufactured in the Northwest so it was available when needed and this helped maintain the mystique of the western steelhead. Still, English imports in rods, reels and flies were found in most respectable shops. Fly rod manufacturers and the fly tying market began to specialize in equipment and materials for western waters. Even though the procurement of certain materials was difficult in the west shops and guides were providing their clients with hybrid patterns. During the early part of the 20th century tiers were beginning to develop steelhead patterns of their own. John Benn, one of Eureka, California's first commercial tiers, began tying patterns for northern California steelhead around 1890. Mr. Benn introduced his Benn's Coachman around the turn of the century and was involved in the development of a good number of early Eel River patterns.

Standard featherwing trout patterns became the basis for many early steelhead flies. Parmachene Belle, Scarlet Ibis and other notable patterns were tied in slightly larger sizes for western ironheads. Many other flies were the result of altering an Atlantic salmon or English trout pattern by substituting or eliminating some of the more exotic materials. Steelhead versions of Durham Rangers and Jock Scotts were showing up in fish camps, along with steelie-sized, trout featherwinged flies and were working on these western fish. When the hairwinged patterns became popular, shortly after the depression, many of these classic featherwing flies began to take a back seat.

The prerequisite for many of the first steelhead patterns seemed to be the popular colors of red and/or white with peacock herl somewhere. Virtually all of the coachman patterns fell into this category along with several other period patterns including the notable Van Zandt, developed by Josh Van Zandt from Eureka, California.

Atlantic salmon patterns also contributed to the development of our first steelhead flies. A popular salmon pattern of the era was the Kate. It was used in its original form for some time and also spawned many other patterns. In 1867, *A Book on Angling*, by Francis Francis, described the Kate as a "new pattern". Its originator is thought to be Mrs. Courtney who was one of the few women who developed salmon flies at that time. George Kelson and Sir Herbert Maxwell helped popularize the Kate in its homeland and by the time it found its way to the United States, around the turn of the century, many variations of this colorful pattern were found.

Steelhead versions of the Kate were quite popular into the 1930's and some simplified versions still remain. Joseph D. Bates, Jr., in his book *Streamer Fly Tying and Fishing*, relates a story which concludes that the Kate was the forerunner to the Railbird.

The Railbird was a common pattern on the Eel River in the early days of steelheading. While the coloring of the two patterns is similar, some feel this is a far stretch. Bates' story tells of Martha Benn being sent a Kate, of some sort, and producing the pattern that is now known as the Railbird, with a few minor changes. Others believe that it was Martha's father, John, that developed the Railbird several years earlier, around 1900, with no thought given to the Kate. Some mysteries will always remain.

While Eel River fishing and flies progressed, news of other rivers farther north drew some to the Rogue and North Umpqua. Zane Grey, enter stage right.

Many patterns that were used in northern California traveled with adventurous fishermen who traveled north. While these people, including Zane Grey, were not responsible for the fishing or most of the flies on the Rogue and North Umpqua they were responsible for promoting it. Since progress is inevitable you might say Zane Grey was its pawn. There were actually very few patterns that Grey was responsible for helping to develop or promote but the Golden Demon was one.

Although the initial Golden Demon's origin is debatable, we do know that it was brought from New Zealand by Grey in the early 1930s. Grey used it with great success on large trout in New Zealand and at home and the Golden Demon found its way to the steelhead rivers Grey fished. From this pattern came the Silver and Black Demons developed by Jim Pray of Eureka, California, both of which were very well accepted on the Eel and produced many fish. Again we go back to the Eel River.

Jim Pray tied flies for the Eel River from the 1930s on, helping to introduce and develop the use of hairwing flies. His hairwing versions of the Railbird and the Improved Governor, with his unique style of short hooks and long wings, were essential in the development of today's hairwing flies. Pray also developed the optic series of flies which used hollow brass beads clamped on the hook and painted eyes. Jim used these flies for the deep holes on the Eel and they became a symbol of sorts to many steelhead fishermen. Pray also helped to originate many other patterns, some of which are still in use today. The Thor, Silver Demon and Black Demon are a few of his surviving patterns.

Back again to southern Oregon and its many local tiers. Both the Rogue and the Umpqua were thriving in the 1930's and 1940s with their fishing and fish camps. The 1930s brought the same style of featherwing patterns that were dominant in the Eel River area of the 1800's. By the 1940s the Rogue showed its own roots in the style of fly evolving in the area. Small, size 8-12, double hooks were common and the trademark wing, upright with divided hair, took hold. The Red Ant, Silver Ant, Fools Gold and Rogue River Special were all standards on the Rogue during this period.

During this time, up north in the Umpqua, the Steamboat legacy was growing and so was the list of North Umpqua patterns. Although there is much history of the North Umpqua in the early 1900s, most of the fly history on this river didn't begin until the early 1930s. It was in the mid 1930s that Clarence Gordon began running fish camps on the North. Around 1937 Clarence developed the Black Gordon which I feel is one of the best all-around dark patterns. Clarence developed other patterns that would not maintain their popularity over the years, nonetheless they were valuable in their day. One pattern that Gordon was involved in developing was the Cummings Special. Ward Cummings was one of many guides that worked the North River in the 1930s. He teamed up with Clarence and a bottle of spirits to develop the Cummings Special which has passed the test of time on the Umpqua and throughout the Northwest.

The Umpqua Special was another pattern of the same era that some feel Clarence had a hand in developing. Vic O'Bryan, another Umpqua guide and fish camp operator, along with Don Harter have also been given credit for this pattern which closely resembles the Rogue River Special. One thing that most Umpqua River patterns had in common was their wool or chenille bodies and hairwings, most of these patterns fall into the same style category. Other patterns of the time given Umpqua River credit are the reliable Skunk, a pattern that Mildred Krogel may have introduced in the late 1930s, and the Stevenson Special, a featherwing fly that Clive Stevenson developed during the 1940s. Although the Stevenson Special has lost much of its following it still remains a good summer pattern and with the resurgence of featherwing patterns may draw renewed interest.

Although not reported with the same vigor, a situation most locals were happy with, Washington state was booming in the steelheading game. What Eureka was to northern California, Seattle became to Washington. Local sports editor and writer, Enos Bradner wrote of local angling in his column appearing in the *Seattle Times.* 1937 was the year that Bradner introduced his Brad's Brat and it was accepted quite well. Enos helped establish the Washington Fly Fishing Club and became a fixture in Northwest fly fishing history.

The same period of time also produced quite a few patterns from the father and son team of Ken and George McLeod. The McLeods introduced us to several important patterns from the 1930s through the 1940s. The Purple Peril's introduction in the late 1930s or early 1940s opened up the violet end of the color spectrum to steelhead fishermen. Actually we probably have Herter's to thank, too. The story has it that younger George ordered some claret materials for dad but they came in very purple. The result of this error was the Purple Peril as we know it. Up to that point purple was almost unheard of in steelheading circles. We would have eventually caught on to the violet colors, but these historical stories make steelheading even more enjoyable.

In 1940 the Skykomish Sunrise was introduced and began taking fish right away. This fly produced several record and award winning fish from the Kispiox from 1955 to 1959.

Among them was a 29 pound, 2 ounce world record rainbow trout. This pattern has special meaning to me because it was the first steelhead fly I ever tied and fished, when I was only 10. I fished it on the South Platt River in Colorado where I grew up. I caught the largest trout of my childhood on this river on an outing with my dad. We didn't catch many fish but I did see my first herd of big horn sheep, less than a hundred yards away. A day memories are made of.

After World War II fly tying was introduced to another material. Shortly after the war, according to Alec Jackson, the use of fluorescent materials began. The story states, that Wes Drain, Anson Brooks and Doc McMahon each purchased a pair of the new hot-colored swim trunks, all in different colors, and unravelled the shorts for material to tie fluorescent flies. Although these new colors were available, in some form or another, in the late 1940 to early 1950s, according to Joe Howell their popularity didn't gain full strength until the 1960s. Gantron was one of the early names for these new materials and later other forms, floss, chenille and wools, were available under the name Ray Depth. These materials and colors helped add to the steelhead fly fisherman's arsenal. The development of fluorescent colors was a major advancement for tying steelhead flies. Although many tiers do not use fluorescents in great amounts, most tiers agree that it adds potential for a great number of patterns.

Washington state produced several important fly tiers during these years but one of the most notable was the late Syd Glasso. Syd has had more written about him than almost any tier in this century. His effect on the quality of today's tiers is hard to measure but is quite obvious. Around 1950 Mr. Glasso started experimenting with an ancient style of fly native to the Spey River in Scotland. Eric Traverner's book, *Salmon Fishing*, was the basis for much of his learning on the Spey fly. Syd started using the traditional Spey flies of the mid-1800s, possibly the Grey Heron, Lady Caroline, Carron and the like, to get a feel for the movement of this style. He incorporated the new fluorescent colors, floss and dyed seal fur, into this unique fly creating a group of flies that became the foundation for the Spey fly patterns dressed by a growing number of today's talented artists. Syd's talents weren't restricted to his graceful Spey flies, his full-dressed Atlantic salmon flies incorporated the same style and meticulous craftsmanship and at this timedemand some of the highest prices known for a modern day tier.

Throughout the 1960s and 1970s history continued. Syd Glasso was developing his style of steelhead Spey fly, probably the first to use this type of fly for steelhead. Mr. Glasso's work on the Spey fly broke the ground for a great many other sculptors of fur and feather. The Spey fly is the epitome of the graceful steelhead fly. Many tiers have since expounded on the classic Spey fly that Syd Glasso and Dick Wentworth made popular.

Not only was his use of the Spey fly for steelhead unique, his methods for applying the materials on these patterns were also trendsetting. Syd Glasso was a pioneer in the use of materials to both build the body and do the tying. He used floss as the tying material and also dubbed on it. He used as few wraps of thread as possible to do the job. By dressing the fly fairly thin he could get the fly to sink better, especially with the silk lines he was using during the time he was developing these flies. The use of hackles for wings on Spey flies was a "new" application at the time, traditional Spey flies almost exclusively had bronze mallard strips for the wings. Although I never met the man, I, and a great many tiers, owe much to Syd Glasso.

As we head north to British Columbia we learn even less about the flies of early time periods. Because of the English influence many early fishermen used traditional Atlantic salmon patterns and developed patterns from these. The B.C. rivers today are much like the southern rivers of the early 1900s. Many of these rivers are seeing their history being made now. The Sustut, for example, was unknown to the majority of anglers until fairly recently. Without the help of aircraft many such fisheries could not be fished, today or then.

Tommy Brayshaw, General Noel Money and Roderick Haig-Brown were instrumental in the early days of Canadian steelheading. Among the things they had in common was their British background and their love for fly fishing and the rivers they fished. The "new" frontier, British Columbia, drew many British citizens in the 1920s and 1930s. For some, General Money included, the fresh, clean environment was a refuge from their ailments.

Because of their British roots many flies that these men developed had a basis in the Atlantic salmon flies of the 1800s and early 1900s. Tommy Brayshaw's Coquihalla series showed definite signs of the early salmon patterns substituting some of the rare feathers. General Money's patterns, on the other hand, had a closer connection to the simple featherwing trout patterns that were associated with the early British Empire. Slim bodies and simple strip wings were common on Money's flies.

Yet without a doubt, Roderick Haig-Brown had the most everlasting effect of all early Canadian fishermen and tiers. His Golden Girl, some feel, was a takeoff on the classic Durham Ranger but the only connection is the golden pheasant wings. The body, hackle and tail are not related to the Durham Ranger in any way, shape or form but may be similar to the Gold Ranger. The Steelhead Bee, with its nontraditional forward wings, was the forerunner to many surface skaters and damp flies. Haig-Brown's writings set him up for generations of admiration from fly fishermen. His poetic style of writing helped set him apart from the many fishing authors of the century.

With the pursuit of wily old steelhead becoming so popular, other modern pioneers began using their skills and resources of new materials to set the stage for more steelhead fly developments.

In many aspects we are seeing history being made now in steelhead angling. People like Alec Jackson, who hasn't been afraid to break the traditions of his fishing partners of the past, are constantly using their ingenuity to develop new methods and uses for old materials. Alec is the perfect example of the blend from past to present. His gentlemanly values and class, matched with his willingness to help and experiment, have helped to bring steelheading up a notch. Although I do not know Alec well, my contact with him through the Northwest Fly Tiers Expositions and while researching this book have convinced me that Alec is a part of steelheading's heritage.

Many unknown tiers are waiting in the wings to share their skills and ideas, along with the many young well-known artists of today. Until the sport is dead and gone the history of the steelhead fly never stops, we just keep adding new pages, in other words, to be continued . . . "

2
Style

THE TERM STYLE HAS A DOUBLE MEANING IN FLY tying. Style can refer to the different character that each individual tier applies to their flies. This is shown in the fact that each tier will tie the same pattern differently. No two tier's are the same, so consequently no two flies are exactly the same.

Each tier must develop his or her own style and then refine it. Often a tier's style may take very long, even years, to perfect. Many notable tiers' works are easily recognized, as is the style they helped to develop. Syd Glasso, with his very slim bodies and tiny heads, helped establish a level of perfection that most tiers have not achieved. This is not to say that this level has not been surpassed for there are several tiers, few as they may be, that have exceeded Glasso's benchmark of excellence.

Many tiers try to imitate the work of other tiers but the flies are never quite the same. Each tier is limited to his or her skills, eye and knowledge of methods and materials. Skills can be honed but the eye for detail and proportion is, I feel, something you are born with. Material knowledge is a learned process that extends far beyond just learning how to handle feathers. The knowledge of materials also extends to knowing what to look for in materials and where to find them. This takes association with other people and contacts to find suitable materials.

The other meaning of style is the type of fly being tied. Compare a standard wet steelhead fly and a Spey fly, these flies are different styles yet they are both effective steelhead flies. The steelhead wet fly has a sturdy utilitarian appearance. Early flies of this type were often tied on heavy hooks and were generally bushy looking. Dick Wentworth and the late Syd Glasso were greatly responsible for initiating the Spey fly into steelheading. Their steelhead versions of this ancient and historical style of fly are quite different from the old standard Bucktail Skunk.

The steelhead fly can be broken down into several different categories of style. Some categories can be divided even further. Some advocate that these "sub" categories warrant a heading of their own but the small number of these patterns don't really justify it.

For a point of reference I separate the flies into four style groups: standard wet, dry/damp, Spey and imitators.

The standard wet fly is the style of steelhead fly that is most common. It includes the bucktail wet fly that we all know and love; the fly that most of us grew up with. While the hairwing steelhead fly may not seem unique to us, it does have its place in the fly tying world. It is special because of its compact design intended to get down to where "Mr. Big Fish" hangs out. These flies include the famous Royal Coachman, Skunk and the Polar Shrimp. These standard flies are normally made with a simple body and tail, the standard wet fly throat hackle and a hairwing, very basic yet very effective.

In the early days of steelheading with a fly, fish were plentiful and not always as particular as they are 80 years later. Over the years water conditions have also changed. Water volumes in the summer have decreased while temperatures have increased resulting in fish not so dead set against coming to the surface for a fly early in the season. So in turn the compact, sometimes fast sinking, bucktail fly has become less popular with many fishermen. With some anglers using floating fly lines year-round the standard bucktail fly has given way to many sparser dressed flies for summer fish but the popularity of the stocky bucktail fly remains strong.

In this group I also include streamers. A streamer is similar in design except that the wings are made of hackle tips. This type of wing provides a good silhouette and desirable movement. Along with the added action these flies are quite compact and sink well without the lead wire underbody, making them great flies for dry line fishing. The drawback to these flies is that they don't always hold up well because the fish's teeth tear up the featherwing. While streamers are popular for some Eastern trout fishing they have never received the same respect in steelhead fishing. There are, however, several streamers that have proven quite successful for steelhead over the years. The Spruce fly, Silver Hilton and Winter's Hope are but a few.

Low water flies also fall into this group. A low water fly is designed to be fished in . . . low water, surprise!!!! When the water temperature drops and the water is very clear, fish tend to get spooky and often shy away from large flies. As we begin to notice droughts and low water conditions year after year we need to provide larger spaces in our fly boxes for low water flies. The North Umpqua, for example, has been experiencing low water levels as early as the end of June in recent years. During few winters there was times when the water level was comparable to July or August. Even though these colder water temperatures make fish hug the bottom, in most cases a sparse, smaller fly can be quite effective. The low water fly is most often tied on smaller, fine wire hooks. Many manufacturers make their low water hook shank slightly longer also.

The fly itself is tied more sparsely and generally not of the same proportions as a standard fly. For example, if we take a size 2 low water hook and tie the fly as though it were on a size 6 hook we would have a basic low water fly. The low water fly may start 1/3 to halfway up the hook from the bend. By doing this the fly is smaller and more sparse. The proportionately larger hook provides the weight on the fly without lead to get it down while using a floating line, which is easier to control and mend.

In low water conditions fish sometimes strike short on the fly. With the hook protruding from the rear of the fly many of these short takes become solid hookups.

Most wet flies can be dressed low water style but simpler flies dress better with less bulk. Some good low water patterns are the March Brown, Summer Twilight and the Red Ant.

The dry/damp style group is a little confusing because some patterns are interchangeable in each of the categories.

Dry flies vary considerably in design. The standard hairwing dry fly, such as the Wulff series, is known by both trout and steelhead fishermen. Clipped deer hair body flies, like the Irresistible and Bomber series, are versatile because they can be fished dry or damp. Another clipped hair body fly, the Umpqua Tailwalker, is very effective but falls into a special class known as a skater. A skater is a dry fly that can be skated on the surface of the water, preferably causing a lot of commotion. While skaters are not completely new to steelheading their usefulness and popularity are on the increase.

Many standard trout dry flies have been modified slightly to accommodate the steelhead fisherman. The first, and most important, change is the size of the fly. With few exceptions,

most anglers do not intentionally fish for steelhead with a size 18 Black Gnat. But tie that fly on a size 8 hook, put a white hairwing and stiff, dark moose hair for the tail, tie the hackle a bit fuller and you have a very effective steelhead dry fly. Other trout dry flies adapted to steelhead fishing are the Fire Coachman, Humpy and many of the Irresistible series.

Damp flies work on the water's surface or just under it. They often are supposed to represent a drowning bug and are effective when fished with a lot of action, such as a riffling hitch. Any dry fly that becomes water-logged is automatically a damp fly and many flies are designed to be fished in that method. A successful damp fly should have enough buoyancy to keep it within a few inches of the surface yet enough weight to stretch the surface film of the water to its breaking point. Once the fly breaks that film it becomes more visible and detailed to the fish.

The Spey fly's long, flowing body hackle and slender body is easy to recognize. The Spey fly has begun to receive greater attention over the last 20 years or so. These flies are generally characterized by their body (Spey) hackle which is often over twice the body length. This hackle, which used to be mainly heron, or the now nearly extinct Spey cock, should be soft and provide a lot of movement. Blue-eared pheasant and other substitutes including schlappen and goose flank feathers now dominate Spey flies.

The hooks for these flies are generally a lighter wire than the standard wet fly hook with a more graceful bend, such as the Partridge Bartleet and Alec Jackson Spey Hooks. The lighter wire provides a good slender base over which to form the petite body of floss, tinsel and seal fur.

Narrow strips of goose shoulder, swan substitute or hackle tips are the norm for the wings on Spey flies but many of the newer Spey flies have more complicated wings. These contemporary Spey flies with wings of golden or amherst pheasant tippets, tragopan pheasant breast feather and hooded merganser, help to make the Spey fly the most striking of all steelhead flies.

Early Spey hooks were quite long, 4-6X long, and made of finer wire. Today, true Spey hooks are all but nonexistent. Some tiers of traditional Scottish Spey flies, including myself, have begun making traditional Spey hooks for those special flies and they really change the appearance.

During the writing and editing of this book, I was rebuked for some patterns that I included in this category. The inclusion of Dee strip wing patterns in this group is sacrilege to some. The Dee strip wing patterns should have their own heading but the small number of flies I received would not allow for that. The distinct difference between these two groups is explained in the Spey fly chapter. But like many other people I lumped them into the same group of flies, those with long body hackles.

The Eagles are another style that fell victim to the same reasoning. Their unique body hackle style makes them very attractive to some and just plain ugly to others. Their wing design is similar to the Dee and different from the Spey. The Eagles represented in this book do not follow the classic lines of the early Eagles yet the basic premise of the soft fluffy hackle still applies.

The notion that certain colors are better in certain rivers, be it correct or not, has lead to the evolution of the steelhead Spey. Our Spey flies have very little in common with the traditional Speys of the 1800s. If the current selection of materials had been available to the fishermen of the River Spey would the flies they used have been drastically different? Possibly. But speculation gets us nowhere. The complete study of Speys, Dees and Eagles, then and now, could be the subject of another book.

The final group of flies I refer to as imitators. While there are flies in all of the previous groups that imitate food in a steelhead's diet this group is reserved for nymphs, prawns, shrimp and leech patterns.

Nymph fishing for steelhead is much like fishing for trout though on a somewhat larger scale. One of the most popular nymphs for steelhead is a version of the stonefly nymph. Stoneflies and salmonflies are a very important part of the steelhead's food chain. Fishing a weighted stonefly nymph can be effective in both summer and winter. Caddisfly pupae fished at the right time and under proper conditions can also provide fishermen with a lot of excitement.

When Colonel Esmond Drury first developed the General Practitioner for Atlantic salmon in the 1950s, he had no idea what he had accomplished for steelhead fishermen. From this fly several patterns have evolved using his general design of multiple shellbacks and long antennae. While Colonel Drury's flies were tied on hooks from size 2 to 6 today's versions are often tied larger, up to 6/0 and 8/0, when the hooks are available. These larger flies are suitable for winter dry line fishing. Dec Hogan's Tragoprawn and Winter Prawn are fine patterns that take off on the General Practitioner style. Although it is an Atlantic salmon pattern, the General Practitioner is still a popular steelhead fly in some circles.

There are other varieties of imitators, such as leeches, which are used frequently on our steelhead streams. Even when there are no real leeches in the water these flies are effective. Leech patterns are most often dark colored and tied with materials that provide a lot of action, such as marabou or rabbit strips. Weighted and fished deep these flies are deadly almost year-round.

While the style of these flies are different they are all steelhead flies and their function is the same: to catch fish. These styles are based on construction only. The choice of materials for a particular pattern may vary drastically from one tier to the next. For instance, when I first began tying the Purple Peril I had only seen it tied with a purple floss body and deer hairwing and fished as a damp fly. Now many shops sell this fly tied with a purple chenille body and squirrel tail wing to be fished weighted as a wet fly. Both are Purple Perils and both have the same basic color scheme. The skunk is another pattern which is often tied in several different styles—wet, low water and as a Spey fly. The construction techniques change but the basic colors remain the same.

3
Materials

MATERIAL SELECTION FOR EARLY STEELHEAD fly tiers was quite slim in comparison to what we have available today. If you had a stock of chenille, wool, floss, dyed hackle, hair for wings and a little tinsel and peacock herl you were pretty well set. The only rare material used regularly was jungle cock. Things were much simpler then, maybe a little drab, but simple.

The steelhead fly tier today has many options that our previous counterparts did not. The introduction of fluorescent materials, shortly after World War II, was one of the first steps into the new world of "modern" synthetics. Gantron and Ray Depth were two of the first names associated with the new hot colors. Wools, chenilles and flosses were available after a time and became quite popular with the winter steelhead crowd.

On the synthetic front things began to explode with the introduction of Mylar products in the 1970s. Later, Flashabou, Krystal Flash and a few other new materials left their lasting mark on the steelhead angler. These materials offered color, flash and movement all in one material. Wings were the main benefactor of these flashy accents but some tiers found other uses for the new synthetics.

A little later braided Mylars were used on bodies as substitutes for tinsels and other standard body materials. By combining all of these interesting materials into some of the standard patterns you create a Buck Rogers look to some old, traditional patterns.

Much of what we now have is a direct result of the craft industry. What is now commonplace in the fly shop was first discovered by a fly tier with foresight. I am always glad to browse through the craft department with my wife, never knowing what I might find. Often she ends up poking me in the ribs saying, "Isn't it time to go yet?"

For quite some time the steelhead fly tier was kind of forgotten by the feather dealers and raisers. The demand for high-quality dry fly hackle birthed a new generation of superior grade "super chickens". These birds had long, narrow hackles for tiny dry flies and the trout angler was delighted but at the same time steelhead anglers were having a hard time finding dry fly hackle large enough for the big Wulff patterns. Recently the demand for large hackle was heard by a few shops and they began searching for these feathers for the steelheader.

While no hair or feather is really "new", many were not used for fly tying until recently. Many pheasants that are in demand now were virtually unheard of by fly tiers twenty years ago. Yet they were always around, at least in the wild. Because of the innovation of some tiers birds such as the blue eared pheasant, tragopan and peacock pheasant are now used when the feathers are available.

The sections below discuss the basic materials you need and some of the more exotic furs and feathers that you might keep an eye out for.

Hair for Wings

Calftail, or kiptail, is a useful hair for wings. The natural color is white but it can be found dyed in all colors. It has a somewhat kinky texture and a translucent appearance. It is a solid hair and has no air pores, so it will sink quite well.

Calftail does not compact well under thread tension sometimes resulting in a larger head than you may want. Also, the wing may be harder to secure, sometimes resulting in a less durable fly. When working with calftail, using it a little sparsely still gives you a full wing and it will tie nicer.

The tail from the Northern whitetail deer is probably the most common form of bucktail hair used for wings on steelhead flies. The hair is long relatively straight and ties well. It is a hollow, porous hair and does not sink as well as calftail. It holds in place and ties a nice, neat head. Bucktail stacks more nicely than calftail and provides a more even wing, it has very little underfur. Bucktail is available in natural white and many dyed colors. When tying dry flies bucktail works well for wings and tails because it is fairly stiff and helps the fly float.

Bear hair is also used for wings on steelhead flies. Most commonly you find black bear hair which is very shiny and quite nice to work with. Most bear hair has a lot of underfur and must be combed out before it can be stacked. This can be done with an underfur comb or a child's toothbrush. Black bear hair comes in different textures and consistencies; I prefer fairly fine hair which makes a more mobile wing. Brown bear hair is a good substitute for brown bucktail because it does not float and has a natural sheen which is lacking in bucktail. Brown bear colors vary from a light cinnamon to a dark rich brown. In the period from the 1940s through the 1960s, another popular hair was the silver-tipped grizzly bear. A good hide had soft, rich brown hair with light tips, cream to golden yellow. This was a beautiful hair but it is hard to find today.

For many years the main wing material used on steelhead flies was polar bear hair. This naturally translucent hair had a glow and sparkle that was nice and these qualities remained even after it was dyed. I find it a little difficult to tie most polar bear because it is a hard and stiff hair but it does tie a nice wing. The shorter hair from around the mask and hair off the paws and lower legs are more fine and the best to tie with.

The availability of polar bear hair is slim to none and dealers that do have it fetch a hearty price for it. After 1968 many of the furs and feathers used for tying became illegal, polar bear is one of them. Occasionally, legal, documented polar bear hair shows up. In 1990 I had a salesman offer me legal polar bear hair for $4.00 per square inch, that is over $550 per square foot and that was a wholesale price! To be legal, my understanding is, the bear had to have been killed prior to 1968 and documented as such. A lot of the polar bear hair that is available is of poor quality with broken tips. High quality polar bear hair is very scarce.

Another fine wing hair is Rocky Mountain goat. Although most people will never see mountain goat hair it is well worth mentioning. Goat hair is similar to polar bear hair in its texture and color but ties a nicer wing, in my opinion. A whole goat skin has a limited amount of prime hair, but that prime hair is exceptional. The best goat hair is fairly fine and very white. Some of it measures up to four inches long. Occasionally it will be offered for sale in a small fly shop somewhere; don't pass it up.

Squirrel tail provides a great deal of useable material for steelhead flies. The Eastern gray squirrel, the red fox squirrel, natural black squirrel and the large Northwest silver-gray are used extensively. The hair is fine and stacks well making a nice, even wing. As a result of its texture a small amount of hair makes a full wing and a clean, small head.

The red fox squirrel can be a favorable replacement for brown bucktail on low water flies, allowing a good sink rate without a lead wire underbody. Red fox squirrel tail is called for as a wing on many summer steelhead patterns, namely the Red Ant and the low water Purple Peril.

The Eastern gray and the Northwest silver-gray can often be used interchangeably. Eastern gray squirrel tails are about half the size of the silver-gray's tails and its hair is shorter and straighter. The Eastern gray has tan markings at the base of the hair while the silver-gray does not. Tied as a wing they both are gray with white and black tips. On smaller summer patterns the silver-gray hair may be too long with the bars being excessively wide, yet there are several patterns that specifically call for silver-gray squirrel.

From time to time natural black squirrel tails are available. They have an interesting dark greenish-black color with darker black bars and slightly lighter tips. This tail is useful on patterns that call for black wings, providing extra character that plain black hair does not.

Squirrel tails are available in many dyed colors. These are used when a slightly somber, buggy dyed hair is desired or a more natural effect is important. Dyed-black squirrel tail makes the sleekest, finest black hairwing I have ever seen. Chuck Gilbert's SSS (steelhead, seal and squirrel) fly uses many different colors of dyed squirrel tail.

The gray fox has some useful hair on its back and tail which is used for wings on several flies, such as the Railbird and the Atlantic Salmon Rat series which double well on steelhead. The tails have long hair and may not be quite what you need for tying today's steelhead flies. Jim Pray used tail hair when tying his Railbird but his style used extra long wings tied on a short shank hook. The guard hairs down the center of the back are best for most steelhead flies, the length is quite a bit shorter and the color is nicer.

I once had some fox tails sent to me by a supplier that were labeled as silver fox. They were almost jet black in color with the very tip of the tail being white. There were a few silver-gray hairs mixed among the black. These made attractive black wings.

By far, my favorite white hairwing material is Arctic fox tail. This hair has quite a bit of underfur that must be combed out prior to stacking but the end result is an even, nearly perfect, snow white wing. The hair is quite fine and will tie a neat head. These tails are a little smaller in comparison to the large gray fox tails so the size of the fly tied is not going to be as large as what one could tie with bucktail. An Arctic fox tail has at least twice as much useable white hair as bucktail so the price, normally about double that of bucktail, is easily justified. This is the only white hair I use on smaller flies, size 2 and under. Dying these tails is difficult as the skin tends to fall apart during the process. By cold dying, at temperatures under 100°, you can get fairly good color but it takes time and the colors are somewhat softer, not quite as bold.

The use of deer hair dry flies has become increasingly popular over the last several years. Fishermen have been working on the skill of "skating" flies and developing special patterns just for this purpose. Due to the increase in popularity of skaters and wakers, the use of deer hair and other buoyant hairs has increased.

Three major American deer species, mule, whitetail and coastal blacktail have useable body hair for wings, spun heads and bodies. I have found from personal experience that blacktail deer does not spin as well as other hairs. The exception is a blacktail hide in prime winter condition. Blacktail deer hair is prized for its mottled appearance and even, fine texture, many tiers find it exceptional for winging dry and damp flies. When you do find a good winter hide, keep it. For spinning heads and bodies coarse mule or Eastern whitetail will do an exceptional job. A heavy winter hide from any type of deer has a considerable amount of underfur which must be removed before tying. Normally, I use a heavier thread when spinning hair. A 3/0 thread works well as do the newer Kevlar threads.

Caribou is another porous hair which spins and flares quite well, making good heads and spun bodies. Its color is generally grayish to light brown and quite solid. It floats like a cork and works extremely well for skaters and dry flies. It can be somewhat brittle because it is so porous.

The light tan and dark brown hair of elk are almost a requirement for wings and tails on many dry flies. If a person had an entire elk hide they would have an amazingly wide variety of colors and textures, all from the same animal. The quality of this hair varies greatly depending on the area and time of year it was taken. While most elk hair is not exceptional spinning hair it does work well on tails and bullet head stonefly patterns.

Every tier should have a nice piece of dark, brownish-black moose hair on hand. Dark moose hair stacks evenly and is one of the only hairs stiff enough for tails on big bushy steelhead dry flies, size 4 and larger. The tanning process removes most of the natural oils from moose that help this hair float so well. Ideally, a moose hide that has been naturally dried, and not tanned, is best suited for surface flies. Heavy thread is a must to successfully spin moose hair. It is extremely coarse and will pack very tight to give a cork-like floatability.

Hair from the antelope with its variegated brown, gray and white colors, combined with its floating abilities, make it an adequate hair for spinning. It is a little brittle and breaks easier than most hairs so the tier must be careful. When I was a kid in Colorado my dad tied a Spuddler, a sort of cross between a spruce and a muddler, and always used antelope for the heads.

A good combination of natural and dyed spinning hair will enable the tier to match whatever caddis or stonefly is hatching at the moment. Matching the hatch is not only for the trout fishermen. Summer steelhead surface quite readily to bugs, both natural and imitation. Though most steelhead dries do not provide a good representation of anything in particular, steelhead are very curious and will often check out things creating movement. On many steelhead rivers an angler must use dry flies that can handle rough water, spun hair flies can.

Dubbing Material

Seal fur dubbing undoubtedly makes the nicest dubbed body of any fur. It sparkles and shines, dyes easily and is fairly easy to work with. The problem is that it has become very difficult to obtain due to the conservation efforts aimed at baby seals. Many tiers have begun looking for adequate substitutes for seal fur. Both natural and synthetic alternatives have risen and some are worth incorporating into your flies.

African and Angora goat furs are an acceptable substitute for seal fur. When tied it takes a skilled eye to distinguish goat from seal, good goat that is, some goat fur is coarser than many tiers

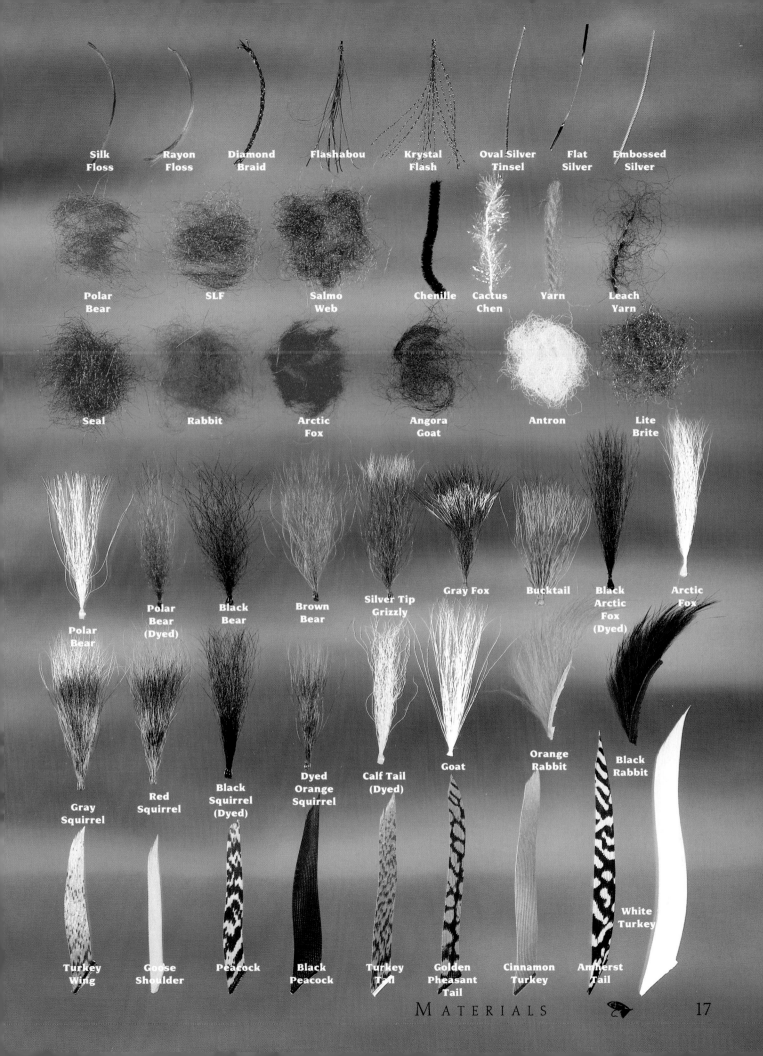

Silk Floss

Rayon Floss

Diamond Braid

Flashabou

Krystal Flash

Oval Silver Tinsel

Flat Silver

Embossed Silver

Polar Bear

SLF

Salmo Web

Chenille

Cactus Chen

Yarn

Leach Yarn

Seal

Rabbit

Arctic Fox

Angora Goat

Antron

Lite Brite

Polar Bear

Polar Bear (Dyed)

Black Bear

Brown Bear

Silver Tip Grizzly

Gray Fox

Bucktail

Black Arctic Fox (Dyed)

Arctic Fox

Gray Squirrel

Red Squirrel

Black Squirrel (Dyed)

Dyed Orange Squirrel

Calf Tail (Dyed)

Goat

Orange Rabbit

Black Rabbit

White Turkey

Turkey Wing

Goose Shoulder

Peacock

Black Peacock

Turkey Tail

Golden Pheasant Tail

Cinnamon Turkey

Amherst Tail

MATERIALS   17

find useable. As for what the difference is between African and Angora goat, I have no idea. I personally think it is in the labeling. They look identical in bulk and when tied. They dye the same and feel the same. When using goat instead of seal the goat should be chopped a little more because the fibers are longer. Another bonus: Angora goat hair is easily obtainable through most fly shops. Some tiers blend what seal they have with goat and receive satisfactory results while making their seal quantity last longer.

There are many good synthetic seal dubs on the market. While most are not realistic seal substitutes they do have some characteristics that are quite nice. Essux Salmo-Web is a long, soft fiber that has a lot of sparkle and when cut short dubs nicely. This material is not to be used on full-dressed Atlantic salmon patterns as a seal substitute, yet it does work well on most fishing flies and retains more sparkle when wet than seal does. SLF, a new synthetic marketed by Partridge of Redditch feels and works very much like seal but, again, has almost too much sparkle to be a good, realistic seal substitute. Additional synthetics such as Antron body dubbing make very nice bodies. While these synthetics don't look like real fur they do make attractive, buggy bodies with lots of sparkle. They tie easily and are available in many colors.

Rabbit fur in its natural and dyed form makes impressive bodies. It is easy to dub plus its soft texture gives the fly a lifelike appearance. For nymph bodies, and bright yet flat bodies, rabbit dubbing is a fishable dubbing. I especially like natural rabbit for clear water patterns because it is less intrusive than sparkled dubbing. A low water March Brown tied with hare's mask dubbing is one of my favorite low water patterns. Blended with other furs, such as goat or Antron dubbing, it makes exceptional bodies.

Hackle Feathers

The most widely used hackle on steelhead flies is saddle hackle found on the lower back of the rooster. Chinese saddle hackle is long and fairly wide with fine stems and is a nice saddle feather. Natural brown, grizzly, furnace and badger are also used to some extent but dyed colors are more commonly used. Practically every color in the rainbow will be represented, including a few not seen in any rainbow. Dyed colors include black, red, yellow, orange, purple, pink, bright blue, dark blue, claret, green, olive, cerise, bleached white plus every fluorescent color imaginable. As I said, every color in the rainbow plus some.

Most bright and fluorescent colors dye best when dyed over white but some dark colors may be dyed over brown and gray. Badger hackle, a black center with light edges, make useable feathers when dyed. Dying feathers is an art that takes years to perfect. Temperature is very important, too much heat will burn your feathers and not enough heat can slow the process and thus the intensity of the color may not be up to par. Cold dying does work but from my experience, which is limited, extra amounts of dye must be used and it takes more time.

My biggest problem with saddle hackle is that I usually end up wasting 1/3 to 1/2 of each feather. When tying large flies saddle hackles aren't always as large as you need. Since it only takes 2 to 3 turns of hackle on most flies, a 7-inch saddle seems like overkill.

Many tiers have started using hen hackles instead of rooster saddles, body feathers from the rooster also work well. These feathers are approximately the same size, shape and texture as Guinea feathers except they can be dyed to any color. Being short and wide there is no waste and the feathers are always wide enough. Furthermore, they're less expensive than premium saddle hackle. Only one small problem: most shops don't know about them in their strung form, finding hen necks is pretty easy. A trend towards softer, more webby feathers has led a lot of tiers to use hen necks and saddles instead of the traditional rooster saddle. Again the fine stem and texture of the feather are well suited to steelhead flies.

The white-spotted black feathers of the Guinea hen are being used more and more for hackles on steelhead flies. When dyed and tied on a fly they produce an interesting throat or collar with a nice break up pattern. On most patterns using Guinea, the feather is tied in by the tip and folded back and no more than a couple of turns are normally used. Its webbiness creates a full collar without a lot of feather.

Pheasants

While researching this book I became aware that there are more types of pheasant than you can shake a stick at. If they were all available we would have a near-endless variety of new feathers to work with. Some birds I discuss are predominant in fly tying while others may be new to many tiers.

The common Chinese ringneck pheasant has been used by tiers for years. The steelhead fly tier also uses this bird in a different way. While some of the body feathers are used in a few patterns, most of what I feel is useable is on the rump and tail. The gray and brown rump patch has long fibered feathers often used on Spey flies for body hackle. They are used both in their natural state and also dyed. The dyed colors are not very bright, due to the natural feather color of gray or brown, however they can be bleached to almost white and the dyed colors are then much brighter. These feathers also work well for long, flowing collars.

The tails on ringneck pheasant provide wing fibers for patterns such as the Doc Spratley and Hardy's Favorite and are also used in some nymph patterns. The natural buggy coloration of these tail feathers provide a creative tier with other options as wings on standard patterns and nymphs alike.

Golden pheasants have been bred for years for their beautiful feathers. The neck is a bright golden-orange with black bars and the crest is a light gold color. The crest is used for tails and toppings for wings on some of the more intricate flies. The neck tippets are used in strands for tails and whole feathers for wings. The neck and crest section is often dyed for use on some newer patterns. General Practitioners tied in dyed colors are very popular, hot orange, red and purple are quite effective. Recently there has been increased use of the red breast and golden rump feathers of these birds for wings, collars and Spey hackles. The tails of these birds are used for underwings on a few patterns and are quite useful.

The Amherst pheasant is the blonde cousin of the golden pheasant, with many of the same markings on the neck. On the Amherst, however, the tippets are white with black bars and the crest is claret colored. I use breast feathers, dyed, for collars and wings, the natural color is white and the texture is nice. The Amherst pheasant isn't used as often as the golden but with a little imagination you never know what you might come up

Golden Pheasant Crest

Partridge

Tragopan Pheasant Neck

Jungle Cock

Grizzly Hen

Hen (Dyed)

Amherst Breast (Dyed)

Peacock Neck

Golden Pheasant Rump

Golden Pheasant Flank

Tragopan Pheasant Shoulder

Red Macaw

Amherst Tippet

Golden Pheasant Tippet (Natural and Dyed)

Teal

Widgeon

Guinea

Tragopan Pheasant Flank

Peacock Pheasant

Silver Pheasant

Silver Pheasant (Dyed)

Hooded Merganser

Gadwall

Woodduck

Barred Woodduck

Bronze Mallard

Dyed Mallard

White-Eared Pheasant Tail

Black Heron

Gray Heron

Blue-Eard Pheasant

Burned Goose Flank

Ringneck Rump

Ostrich Herl

Saddle Hackle

Schlappen

Marabou

Peacock Sword

M A T E R I A L S 19

with. Dyed tippet sections are quite useful on some Spey flies and full-dressed steelhead patterns.

Other exotic pheasants, such as tragopan and peacock pheasants, are used very little in standard flies but a creative tier can find a lot of uses for the unique birds.

I was shown my first tragopan by Joe Howell of the Blue Heron Fly Shop in Idleyld Park, Oregon. I said, "That is really neat but . . ." Joe quickly finished, "Don't ask, 'what can you do with it?'" Joe has a very creative mind and likes to experiment with anything new, usually with good results. The tragopan, or red pheasant, has a deep, rusty-red breast feather with an "eye" in the center, much like the jungle cock. It makes wonderful wings or cheeks.

The blue eared and brown eared pheasants have probably not been seen by a lot of fly tiers. The first blue eared pheasant I had seen was at the Fly Tiers Expo in Eugene, Oregon in 1990. Steve Brocco from Seattle, Washington had one at his table. From across the room I thought he had a blue heron skin on his table. I thought Steve looked more intelligent than to have a heron skin on display. These birds are quite large in comparison to the common ringneck. The main difference between the blue and the brown eared pheasants is the color . . . surprise! The blue eared is actually a blue-gray color, similar to the color of a blue heron. The brown eared is brown, of course, with a few white saddle feathers. The feathers on these birds are large with

long weepy fibers, excellent Spey feathers. These birds are quite rare, with only blue eared skins being available, the price reflects this at well over $100.00 per skin.

Another utilitarian steelhead feather is the common marabou plume. This fluffy feather is available today in almost any color you might want. Also available now is mottled marabou. These feathers have bars of dark brownish tones contrasting the dyed bright colors. The soft, mobile fibers of the marabou plume offer several uses.

Marabou makes an agile wing material. By snipping sections from the tip of a marabou blood quill, the fine stemmed, soft feather, these sections can be tied in as a wing. Several patterns were designed around this method plus it can be used to alter any standard pattern when more mobility is wanted. The addition of a few strands of Krystal Flash or Flashabou as an underwing helps finish off an attractive wing.

By packing sections of marabou mixed with Flashabou or Krystal Flash you get the effect that George Cook achieved on his Alaskabou series. This series of flies are quick to tie and are lifelike in their movement. These flies also give the illusion of bulk and allow the elimination of a body without any detraction. Fishing a Kandy Kane deep and slow for winter fish is very effective.

Marabou as a Spey feather is another bonus of these feathers. The low cost and choice of colors make marabou a good alternative to some of the more expensive or rare feathers. The

marabou needed has a fine texture in the flue area but that is my personal preference. Regardless of the texture you choose, the stem must be as fine and straight as you can get. Because of the softness of this feather most tiers find it desirable to counter-wrap the feather with either fine wire or extra fine oval tinsel to help prevent feather breakage from fishes teeth.

For a fly of moderate fullness I strip one side of the feather away, tying it in by the tip. If you like a fly that is full, similar to the classic Eagle series, leave the feather intact and double it. Some people may feel that marabou is too soft to use as a Spey feather but I feel that in very slow water they are more than adequate.

Duck Feathers

Just 20 years ago the use of duck feathers was limited in steelhead flies. Occasionally a pattern called for a sprig of mallard flank or black and white-barred woodduck for a tail or possibly a collar made of mallard flank. Bronze mallard shoulders were often used as wings on Spey flies and that was about the extent of the use of duck feathers on steelhead flies.

More recently steelhead fly tiers began using other types of duck feathers. Almost any duck species has some useful feathers

for steelhead flies. Normally, flank and shoulder feathers are most frequently used but other feathers are also finding their way into fly tiers favor.

Drakes are the most commonly used duck. Their feathers are not only larger than those found on hens but they are also sought after for their markings. I seldom have use for hen duck feathers but I never turn down a duck skin of any kind.

When processed properly the extra large flank feathers from a drake mallard are useful for body hackles on Spey flies. First burn the flue from the feather with a mixture of liquid chlorine bleach and water, one part bleach to two parts water. Don't let the feather stay in the mixture much longer than one minute and keep the feather moving at all times. Rinse the feather well and it can be dyed easily to any dark color like black, purple or blue. The fairly heavy, stiff stem is a drawback but this can be worked around by not using too much of one feather.

Teal, gadwall and pintail all have a heavy vermiculated black and white barred flank feather which is used for collars, wings and sides on a number of patterns. Gadwall flank is often large enough to use as a Spey hackle. The widgeon also provides nice flank and beautiful shoulder feathers for wings and collars. One of the most regal looking ducks is the hooded merganser. This bird has desirable flank feathers that are used by tiers for sides and wings on a variety of incredible Spey flies.

The woodduck has both black and white-barred feathers and finely marked flank feathers that have been useful for years to trout and salmonfly tiers but have only recently received acclaim with the steelhead fly tier. Instead of using small sections of the golden flank feather for tails and wings for dry flies these feathers work well for veilings on wings and as hackles. The natural black feathers on the back, near the tail, work well for hackles also.

In general, almost any duck will have some useful feathers in either their natural or dyed state. When dying duck feathers extra care must be taken to remove the oily film which helps shed water but prevents the dye from taking. Even the lowly coot, or mud hen, has suitable feathers for Spey flies.

Winging Feathers

Featherwinged flies, which once were the standard, have been replaced with hairwing patterns. Through featherwinged flies never really died they are experiencing a rebirth. Early classic steelhead patterns were often featherwings. The Golden Demon and Royal Coachman were first featherwing patterns. Bronze mallard and white swan or duck strips made up the wings on these two flies. When hairwing flies became popular in the 1930s and 1940s, the popularity of featherwing flies began to wane. With the introduction of Spey flies to steelheading, along with the fact that many rivers no longer have the water flows they once did, featherwing flies rebounded.

Various wing and shoulder feathers are quite common for featherwing flies today. Even though bronze mallard is difficult to work with it still results in an attractive dark featherwing. Other duck shoulders excellent for wings are the American widgeon and gadwall. Hooded merganser, teal and pintail flank feathers also give a nice vermiculated wing.

The contemporary steelhead fly is a blend of many styles, including the Atlantic salmon fly. The married wing style of the salmon fly has carried over into many steelhead patterns. Where our predecessors used dyed swan, goose shoulder is now more common. Shoulder feathers should not be confused with primary or secondary quills, which are much stiffer and wider-fibered, not what you want for streamlined wings. Swan is still available from time to time at a much higher cost than goose

shoulder. Goose is a finer texture than swan, allowing for a slightly smaller head. I dye my goose the same color as my hackles and body materials. I like to have a good variety for Spey flies and low water patterns. Blended strips of married goose shoulder provide an interesting effect, even if only two colors are used.

Mottled oak turkey quills are a must for a good number of strip wing steelhead patterns. Mottled turkey, which used to be quite cheap, is now harder to find. The secondary quills are used for wings and not the primary feathers. These birds lost popularity to the commercial breeders in lieu of the larger breasted white turkey now grown for the table. Consequently the feathers from the mottled turkey became scarce and the price went up.

Even on mottled turkeys there is a large variation in the feathers. Colors ranging from a mottled tan to dark brown and even gray, are found classified as mottled turkey. The size of the feather is not as important to the steelhead fly tier as its quality. Occasionally #2 grade mottled turkey can be found, with its smaller size being the only defect.

Turkey tails are also of use for strip wings. Mottled turkey and the wild Rio Grande variety both tie good wings, provided the quality is there. The early Dee strip wing patterns and the Eagles both used turkey tail for the wings. The Dees used cinnamon, or sometimes white, and the Eagles used mottled tails. Good quality white turkey tails are almost nonexistent today so we are forced to use goose shoulder or turkey round wing feathers when we want a dyed wing. I feel turkey tails are straighter and tie a nicer Dee style wing. Avoid ratty tails without tight edges. Clean tips are hard to come by but the sides are generally good. Use center quilled feathers or matched left and right tails.

Peacock secondary quills, along with hen pheasant tails, will tie strip wings. Peacock quills are marked coarsely, not as finely mottled as turkey. The buff and dark contrast makes a buggy wing on either wet flies or dries, especially caddis imitations. Hen pheasant tails have similar markings, depending on the breed of pheasant, but the smaller size limits the size of fly.

Body Materials

Wools, chenilles and flosses are the primary materials for most bodies on steelhead flies. Spending time in a yarn shop can prove profitable to the tier. Different yarns and blends of wool and synthetics have created some extremely nice yarns. Mohair and Orlon blends, Molon, are the nicest yarns to work with in my opinion. They shine and are fuzzy enough to resemble life. Yarns can be separated to one or two strands to achieve a different fullness on the body.

During the Victorian era of the Atlantic salmon, tiers used Berlin wools. These were a very coarse wool resembling the yarns used in crewel work. They had a hard appearance but the colors were strong.

The use of chenille is on the decline for most of today's new steelhead patterns. While it was the norm for most bodies up to the mid 1970s many current tiers prefer a material with a little more life. When wet, chenille is a pretty dead material. It does, however, provide the illusion of bulk, a desirable quality on heavy winter flies. More often chenille is being replaced with dubbing, yarns and even ostrich herl on many traditional patterns. A little ingenuity goes a long way when adapting a fly to your fishing situation.

Floss gives a slim and trim body for low water summer patterns. Until the last 40 years or so silk was the primary material for floss. After World War II nylon and rayon were seeing action in fly tying floss. Recently silk floss is making a strong comeback. Several Japanese silk flosses are now on the market in the U.S. Although the price is considerably higher for silk than nylon, it does tie a nicer fly. Silk floss does fray from rough hands more than nylon but careful use and maybe a pair of silk gloves will eliminate this problem.

Hooks

Just as there are many different styles of flies there are also many different styles of hooks. The hook is a great determining factor for the style of fly that will be tied. It is difficult to get a dry fly to stay afloat while using a 5X strong Mustad 7970 as the backbone. The first decision when tying a fly is which hook to build it around. Either the style of fly influences the hook you choose or the hook you choose determines the style of fly.

Speaking strictly from a fisherman's standpoint, the hook's main purpose is to get down to the fish (or stay up depending on the fly), hook the fish and hold him. The fisherman's requirements are strictly utilitarian; good, strong wire and a sharp, sticky point will suffice for many fishermen.

The more a person fishes the more he or she will notice other factors in the hooks they use. Some may notice that certain hooks tend to hold fish better than others. Just as fishermen develop preferences on rods they also develop a preference on hooks, whether they tie flies or not. If an angler loses four fish in a row on a certain hook, whether the hook is at fault or not, the hook becomes suspect. Some fishermen may conclude that brand X hooks won't hold a fish but the problem may be in their style of fishing.

The steelhead is a formidable prey and must be looked upon with respect. Fish which reach 30 pounds in some rivers should not be fished for with standard trout gear or hooks. The steelhead fly hook should be strong enough for the savage strikes it may experience yet have a sharp enough point to stick a fish on the lightest of takes. The wire diameter on a hook will vary depending on the situation for which the hook was designed. A large wet fly hook will have considerably heavier wire than the low water or dry fly hook. The wire diameter will also vary from one hook manufacturer to another, even on the same style of hook. A wet fly hook may range from 1X strong to 5X strong depending on the model and maker of the hook.

The most popular steelhead fly hook is probably the black, looped eye salmonfly hook. This type of hook is manufactured by many companies including Mustad, Partridge and Tiemco to name a few. The standard salmon, wet fly hook is normally 1X or 2X strong wire. Low water hooks are usually 1X strong and are slightly longer than a standard wet fly hook. Dry fly steelhead hooks are most often 1X fine wire yet may be as thin as 4X fine with some manufacturers.

Many tiers prefer the standard wet fly hook with a downed ball eye. While this is a personal preference for some there are many flies that do not tie well on this hook. Both Mustad and Eagle Claw make serviceable hooks that fall into this category.

The steel wire that the hook is made from, as well as its diameter have a bearing on the strength of the hook. Some manufacturers prefer that their hooks give a little under strain while others make a hook that will not bend at all but may break instead. A bent hook or a broken hook, the end result is the same: a lost fish. Every maker has their own alloy making their hook unique. I prefer a fairly ridged hook with a high carbon content like the Partridge or Tiemco hooks.

The strength of the hook is of no importance if the point isn't sharp enough to penetrate a fish's jaw. Several years ago the process of chemically sharpening hooks became popular among hook manufacturers and fishermen. Chemical sharpening involves polishing the points with acids, resulting in extremely sharp hooks. The only problem with this, aside from the higher price, is that the process sometimes weakens the point of the hook resulting in a point that may break easier. I guess we can't have our cake and eat it too. I feel a hand-honed needle point as found on many English hooks is the best compromise.

In today's age of catch and release some fishermen prefer a barbless hook. On many rivers and lakes regulations for barbless hooks are the norm, though a good number of fishermen have opted to do this on a voluntary basis for years. When fishing these bodies of water barbs must be either filed off or flattened with a pair of pliers.

When using a barbed hook the size of the barb should be considered. Many hooks have barbs much larger than necessary to hold a fish. This has two drawbacks; first, it makes it harder to get good penetration, second, it is harder to remove without damaging the fish should you wish to release the fish unharmed. A small barb is all that is needed to hold most fish.

The eye of the hook is the spot where you will tie your leader and should be as smooth as possible. This is one of the reasons I prefer a looped eye hook. A closed eye, such as a ball eye, has the chance of a rough spot where the eye closes and therefore may fray the leader. This is very important when using a Duncan loop, or similar knot, to attach your fly because the ball style eye may rub on the loop.

The Japanned black finish on the salmon style hook has become the most predominant finish for steelhead fly hooks. It takes the glare off and is quite durable, provided you don't cast into a pile of rocks. Some people prefer a nickel finish on their hooks, this gives extra flash and is also durable. Alec Jackson has offered his hooks with several finishes including nickel, gold, bronze, black and blue.

The style and shape of the fly is greatly determined by the hook on which it is tied. A beautiful fly starts with a beautiful hook. While the shape of the hook may not be all that important to the fisherman, it should be to the fly tier. A slender Spey fly must be tied on a hook with a graceful bend to get the flowing form that is desired.

The general shape of the salmon fly hook is universal with a few exceptions. The shank may vary from a standard length to 2X long. The shank forms the bend of the hook which is usually some form of Limerick, or what some call the "English salmon bend".

Exceptions to the general salmon shape are the Partridge Bartleet and the Alec Jackson Spey hook, both of which are similar in shape and design. Both have a sweeping curve to the shank but a different bend shape completely. The bend of the Bartleet is shaped after the one hundred year old Bartleet Limerick style of Atlantic salmon fly hook, thus the name. The

Alec Jackson hook's bend is a little less exaggerated and the shank is approximately 1X shorter than the Partridge Bartleet CS 10/1. Partridge also offers their Bartleet in a shorter, stronger hook, the CS 10/2 and a blind eyed version, the CS 10/3. The points and barbs of these hooks are more rakish than a standard hook, providing a very sticky point. All of these hooks tie a graceful fly.

The traditional Spey fly of the past was tied on a longer, fine-wired Dee hook. These hooks were about 4X-6X long and 1X or 2X fine. At the time of this writing, there is not a hook manufactured, to my knowledge, matching these specifications. There are a few custom hook makers who manufacture Dee hooks but these hooks are mainly used by tiers of exhibition salmon flies and are quite expensive.

Low water hooks normally have a slightly lighter wire and the shank should be 2X longer than a standard salmon fly hook. These hooks are used to tie sparser, smaller flies for low, clear water when the fish may be a bit spooky. All of the same structural qualities should apply to these hooks also. The Bartleet and Alec Jackson hooks make fine low water flies.

The looped eye is important in tying many flies. A good many methods of attaching featherwings and hackles cannot be done with a ball eye. Even then, not all looped eyes are the same. A good looped eye will not have squared edges on the end of the wire and should also be slightly open. This allows for a smoother transition from the body to the wing and hackle and also permits the tier to tie in and tie back materials as needed. Some makers of salmon fly hooks, such as Partridge, Tiemco or Alec Jackson's Spey Hook, are quite accomplished in this area. Mustad salmon fly hooks need some serious work in this area.

They say history repeats itself. This is especially true in fly tying. Of the many blind eyed hooks (hooks without an eye) only the fine point is making a comeback. For several centurieshooks had to be tied with a twisted silk gut loop for an eye or snelled prior to tying the fly. Today many tiers are going back to the gut loop style, feeling that the softer transition from the leader to the fly helps the fly swim gracefully. Braided Dacron fly line backing works well for the looped eye instead of silk gut which is hard to find and in comparison to many synthetic materials, not very durable. I often use three strands of eight pound mono and braid them together to form a loop material which is flexible and it looks like the silk gut of years ago. I like to use a soft mono, such as Berkley Trilene or Bagley's Silver Thread. When tying this style of eye, I wrap the shank with a single layer of thread and attach the loop eye and then use a few drops of Super Glue . . . I know, this isn't very traditional but if it was available I am sure many old time Atlantic salmon fly tiers would have used Super Glue.

Other patterns require an extra heavy wired hook, such as Bill McMillan's Paint Brush. The Paint Brush is tied on a Mustad 7970, a hook with a pronounced limerick bend and 5X strong wire. This is a fine hook for winter, dry line steelhead fishing as it sinks well without lead underwire.

For many tiers the search for materials becomes a lifelong quest. While some of the materials discussed are difficult to find they are not necessary for most fly tiers. A person can tie many functional and attractive steelhead flies without going to the expense and aggravation of the "eternal material search". New materials are becoming available all the time and the arsenal of the fly tier grows every year. By increasing your supply of new materials, both natural and synthetic, and experimenting at will, who knows what new killer fly you may develop.

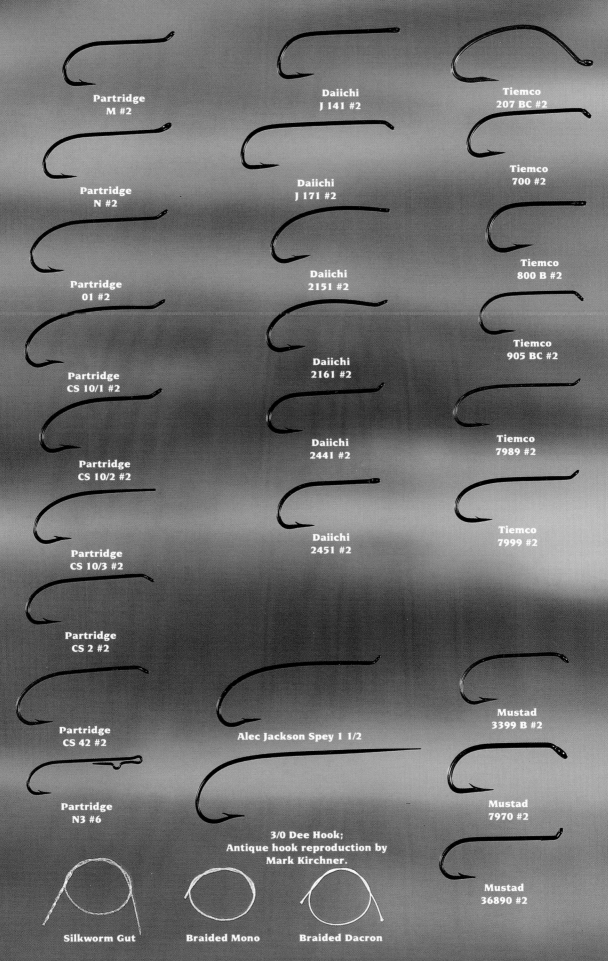

Partridge
M #2

Partridge
N #2

Partridge
01 #2

Partridge
CS 10/1 #2

Partridge
CS 10/2 #2

Partridge
CS 10/3 #2

Partridge
CS 2 #2

Partridge
CS 42 #2

Partridge
N3 #6

Daiichi
J 141 #2

Daiichi
J 171 #2

Daiichi
2151 #2

Daiichi
2161 #2

Daiichi
2441 #2

Daiichi
2451 #2

Alec Jackson Spey 1 1/2

3/0 Dee Hook;
Antique hook reproduction by
Mark Kirchner.

Silkworm Gut

Braided Mono

Braided Dacron

Tiemco
207 BC #2

Tiemco
700 #2

Tiemco
800 B #2

Tiemco
905 BC #2

Tiemco
7989 #2

Tiemco
7999 #2

Mustad
3399 B #2

Mustad
7970 #2

Mustad
36890 #2

4
Wet Flies

THE WET STEELHEAD FLY MAKES UP A LARGE, diversified and important group of dressings. The term wet fly a catch all phrase for those flies that do not qualify as a dry, Spey or prawn, etc. Some of these flies are traditional patterns but many are far from traditional, basic or standard yet they all fall into the same class by a freak chance of fate.

Many of these flies can challenge and test a tier's skill and patience. Their intricate design and unusual use of materials help to make them unique. Others are what many professional fishermen call guide flies, flies that are very effective on the fish and are quick and inexpensive to tie because clients often lose a lot of flies. Big, lead eyed leech patterns are good examples of guide flies but they can be nearly fatal if they hit you in the head.

Graceful low water flies also fall into this group. Many low water patterns are trimmed-down standard flies yet others are sleek flies specifically designed for this type of fishing. Quite often these flies are Atlantic salmon flies which we steelheaders have adapted to our needs. Although they have their own characteristics, these flies are still wet flies. It is hard to put low water flies in their own group because low water is generally a manner in which a fly is dressed rather than a pattern in itself. I will, however, make mention when specific flies are intended to be tied low water fashion or when a good low water dressing is available.

We start with a very simple hairwing steelhead pattern, the Black Prince.

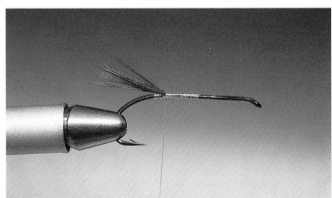

STEP 1: Attach the tying thread to the hook and bring back directly over the point of the hook and tie in a piece of fine oval silver tinsel. Wind it forward five or six turns and tie off.

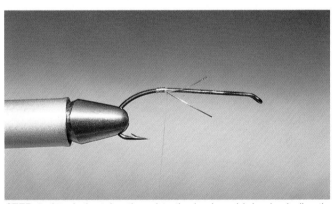

STEP 2: Tie in a small bunch of red hackle fibers slightly longer than the gap of the hook.

STEP 3: Tie in a piece of medium oval silver tinsel and bring the thread forward about a third of the way and tie in a piece of yellow floss.

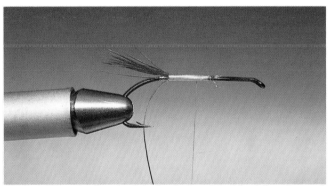

STEP 4: Wrap the floss back to the tie-in point of the tail and wrap it back forward to the tie-in point of the floss and tie it off. Try to keep the floss flat and fairly thin.

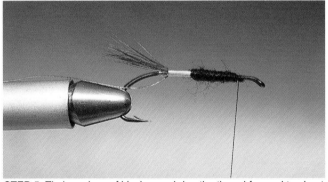

STEP 5: Tie in a piece of black yarn, bring the thread forward to about 3/16 of an inch from the eye. Wind the yarn forward and tie off.

STEP 6: Wind five or six turns of tinsel for a rib, trying to keep them evenly spaced. The number of wraps is subject to your preference.

STEP 7: Take a small bunch of black hair, about half of the total amount wanted for the entire wing, and tie it in with a few *tight* wraps of thread, making sure the ends of the wing come to about the middle of the tail. Add a small drop of thin head cement to the wraps.

STEP 8: Tie in a black hen hackle with the fibers about a gap-and-a-half in length by the tip.

STEP 9: Fold the hackle in half, take three or four turns of hackle and tie it off.

STEP 10: Tie in another small bunch of hair with some tight wraps and cement. Let set a moment.

STEP 11: Wind a fairly small head, whip finish it off and cement. The finished Black Prince.

Another method of tying in a hairwing is shown while tying the Cummings.

STEP 1: Start by choosing a looped eye hook with a smooth eye and a slightly tapered opening towards the eye. Select the brown hair to be used, I chose silver-tipped grizzly for this fly, and cut a small bunch equivalent to the size of the wing and insert it through the eye with the tips up.

STEP 2: Judge the length of the wing by pulling the wing back, it should extend just past the bend. Hold the base of the hair in place and let the wing come back forward then tie in the wing material with the hair pointing forward.

STEELHEAD FLY TYING GUIDE

STEP 3: Bind the wing material down while bringing the thread back to the rear of the hook. Tie in a piece of fine oval silver tinsel for the rib.

STEP 4: Come forward about a third of the way and tie in a piece of yellow floss, wrap it towards the rear and bring it back to the tie in point.

STEP 5: Tie in a piece of claret yarn and bring the thread forward to about an eighth of an inch from the wing. Wind the yarn frontward tightly and tie off.

STEP 6: Bring the rib forward about five or six turns and tie off. Then tie in a claret hen hackle by the tip.

STEP 7: Fold the hackle and take about three or four turns and tie off.

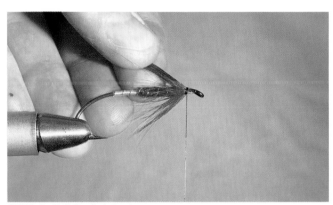

STEP 8: Pull the hair back to the wing position and begin binding it down and forming the head at the same time.

STEP 9: Finish the head and whip finish and cement. The Cummings tied Ed Haas-style is completed.

This style of tying a standard hairwing is preferred by many tiers because of its durability. Learning to get your proportions right on the wing when tying this way takes practice.

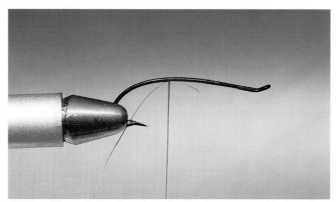

STEP 1: Start with the thread attached in the center and tie in a piece of fine oval gold tinsel and tie it down to the start of the tag, above the point of the hook.

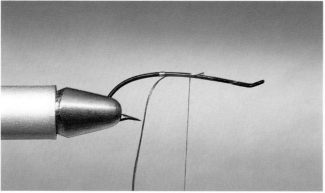

STEP 2: Wind four or five turns of tinsel for the tag and tie off and then tie in a thin strand of red floss.

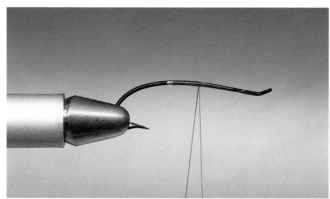

STEP 3: Wrap the floss forward to about the halfway point and tie off and form a dubbing loop.

STEP 4: Dub the remainder of the body with deep purple seal fur or a good substitute, stopping about 3/16 of an inch from the eye.

STEP 5: Tie in by the tip a long, deep purple hackle and take a couple of turns and repeat with a long, golden pheasant rump feather dyed red.

STEP 6: Select a pair of well mottled turkey quills and set them out in front of you. The good sides should be up and they should be curving towards each other. The left quill is for the near wing, if you tie right handed, and the right quill is for the far wing. Cut a matching pair of sections out of each quill about 1/4 of an inch wide.

STEP 7: Hold the near wing section in your right hand with the tip up slightly and gently stroke it straight and slightly downward.

STEP 8: The finished near wing section should look like this. Repeat with the other wing section.

STEP 9: Hold both wings together and place them on top of the fly. Form a soft loop over the top of the wings and bring the thread around a full turn so that you will be tightening the loop with an upward pull.

STEP 10: Gently pull the loop tight. With that upward pull snug, take a couple of wraps after the wing is secured where you want it.

STEP 11: Trim the wing butts, finish off the head and the fly is done.

Plate 1 Page 44

AGENT ORANGE

HOOK: Standard salmon for deep sunk or Alec Jackson Spey Hook for subsurface
BODY: Flat gold tinsel or gold Diamond Braid
WING: A small bunch of fox and squirrel tail enveloped by a pair of golden pheasant tippets
COLLAR: Deer hair spun, Muddler style
HEAD: Deer hair spun and clipped to a cone

Bill May of Roseburg, Oregon developed this pattern and fishes it summer and winter. Bill informs me this fly works well on a floating line, greased line method or sunk deep.

ALEXANDRA

HOOK: Partridge Bartleet Supreme, sizes 2-4
TAG: Red floss
TAIL: Red swan or goose with 3 peacock sword tips over
BODY: Flat silver tinsel
RIB: Fine oval silver tinsel
BEARD: Black hen hackle
UNDERWING: Very small bunch of black bear hair with 2 strips of red swan or goose over
OVERWING: Small bunch; 8-10 peacock swords
HEAD: Black

This version of a 19th century British trout fly was sent to me by Donald Storms of Oak Ridge, New Jersey. Don is an avid fisherman who teaches fly tying for the North Jersey Chapter of T.U. Don was the 1992 Mid-Atlantic Fly Tying Champion.

AMERICAN STEELHEADER

HOOK: Alec Jackson Spey, sizes 1 1/2 or 3, gold
TAG: Fine oval gold tinsel and bright yellow silk floss
TAIL: Two red-tipped golden pheasant crests with toucan substitute over
BUTT: Yellow ostrich herl
BODY: Flat or embossed gold tinsel
RIB: Medium oval gold tinsel
HACKLE: Short yellow, one side stripped, wound along ribs from the second turn of tinsel
COLLAR: Mallard flank dyed yellow
UNDERWING: Yellow goose shoulder
WING: Alternate strips of 7 red and 6 white goose shoulder, starting and ending with red
CHEEKS: Very small guinea feather with kingfisher over
TOPPING: Golden Pheasant crest
HORNS: Blue and gold macaw
HEAD: Three turns of fine oval gold tinsel coated with pearl paint over thread in front
THREAD: Yellow 6/0

Dr. David C. Burns of McCall, Idaho sent me his American Steelheader along with a note. He asked, "Why bother with these complicated patterns? Well, they work 'cause steelhead really aren't too picky . . . and they're pretty! Yes the fish and the flies."

AUTUMN MIST

HOOK: Partridge Bartleet Supreme, sizes 2-4
TAG: Fine oval silver tinsel
BODY: Orange floss
RIB: Fine oval silver tinsel
COLLAR: White Arctic fox followed by orange Arctic fox (this collar is applied by spinning the fur in a dubbing loop and then applying it as a collar)

Donald Storms of Oak Ridge, New Jersey sent this fly along with four others using Arctic fox in the collar and or wing. Spinning fur in a loop gives a lot of movement in a collar or body. Arctic fox gives a little more sparkle than rabbit and is somewhat more durable also.

AUTUMN RUN

HOOK: *Partridge Bartleet Supreme, sizes 2-4*
TAG: *Fine oval gold tinsel*
BODY: *Burnt orange floss*
RIB: *Fine oval gold tinsel*
COLLAR: *Gray Arctic fox (see Autumn Mist)*
WING: *Orange Arctic fox tail*
HEAD: *Black*

This is another of Donald Storms' colorful flies employing Arctic fox for the collar.

BIRDS

Greg Scot Hunt's Bird series consists of the Blackbird, Bluebird and the Firebird. These flies resemble some Atlantic salmon patterns of generations past. Each fly has the same framework yet is remarkably different in color and choice of materials.

BLACKBIRD

HOOK: *Partridge Bartleet, 4-3/0, modified blind eye*
EYE: *20lb braided Dacron loop*
THREAD: *Black 6/0*
TAG: *Fine oval silver tinsel*
TAIL: *Golden pheasant crest with one pair of natural black feathers from the neck of a ringneck pheasant, set upright*
BUTT: *Red wool*
BODY: *In three equal sections; first two are black floss veiled above and below with pairs of black pheasant neck feather set upright and butted with red wool. Third section, black seal fur*
RIB: *Fine oval silver tinsel over each section*
COLLAR: *Natural guinea fowl*
WING: *Black goose shoulder or turkey strips tented semi-Spey style*
HEAD: *Black 6/0 thread*

This pattern was developed by Greg in 1991 for the Babine and Bulkey rivers for late summer fish.

BLUEBIRD

HOOK: *Partridge Bartleet, 2-2/0, modified blind eye*
EYE: *20lb braided Dacron loop*
THREAD: *Black 6/0*
TAG: *Fine oval silver tinsel*
TAIL: *Golden pheasant crest and a pair of blue kingfisher feathers tied upright*
BUTT: *Red wool*
BODY: *In three equal sections; first one is light blue floss, butted with red wool and veiled above and below with pairs of blue kingfisher feathers. Second section is medium blue floss, butted with red wool and veiled above and below with pairs of blue kingfisher feathers. Final section is violet floss*
RIB: *Fine oval silver tinsel over all sections*
HACKLE: *Light blue schlappen behind the ribs over the violet floss*
COLLAR: *Violet schlappen*
WING: *Mottled peacock secondary wing strips*
CHEEKS: *Blue kingfisher*
HEAD: *Black or red thread*

Greg Scot Hunt's Bluebird is a good late summer/early winter pattern. Its blue and purple coloration is good in low light conditions.

FIREBIRD

HOOK: *Partridge Bartleet, 2/0-3/0, modified blind eye*
EYE: *20lb braided Dacron loop*
THREAD: *Red 6/0*
TAG: *Fine oval silver tinsel*
TAIL: *Golden pheasant crest topped with one pair of small tippets dyed red/orange*
BUTT: *Orange wool*
BODY: *Three equal sections; first and second section are fine oval silver tinsel veiled above and below with pairs of dyed red/orange golden pheasant tippets, set upright, and butted between with red wool. The third section is violet seal fur*
RIB: *Fine oval silver tinsel over seal fur only*
HACKLE: *Dyed red/orange pheasant rump over seal fur only, along ribs*
COLLAR: *Dyed violet-purple pheasant rump*
WING: *Dyed violet-purple goose shoulder or turkey strips set Spey style*
HEAD: *Red thread*

Greg Scot Hunt uses this "Bird" fly for winter steelhead around his home in Redmond, Washington and throughout his fishing grounds.

BLACK DEMON

HOOK: *Standard salmon or steelhead hook*
TAG: *Oval gold tinsel, long*
TAIL: *Two sections of barred woodduck flank feather curved upward*
BODY: *Flat gold tinsel*
COLLAR: *Deep orange, stiff saddle hackle wound before wing is applied*
WING: *Black bear or Arctic fox dyed black, full*
CHEEKS: *Jungle cock*
HEAD: *Black*

Around 1937 Jim Pray introduced the Black Demon and Silver Demon for northern California rivers, including the Eel River and the Orleans. Sometimes the Black Demon was tied with a silver body which leaves the wing as the main difference between the two flies.

BLACK GNAT

HOOK: *Low water or Alec Jackson Spey*
TAG: *Fine oval silver tinsel*
TAIL: *Black hen hackle fibers*
BODY: *Black ostrich, twisted with thread to form a chenille*
THROAT: *Black hen hackle*
WING: *Dark slate gray colored goose or duck strips*

Ray Bergman's color plates in his book *Trout* inspired Joe Rossano's Black Gnat. Joe includes this pattern in his American Low Water series.

Plate 2 Page 45

BLACK GORDON

HOOK: *Standard salmon or steelhead hook*
BODY: *Rear 1/3 red floss or wool; front 2/3 black wool*
RIB: *Oval gold tinsel*
COLLAR: *Black hen or saddle hackle*
WING: *Black hair: bear, bucktail, etc.*

The Black Gordon is a native North Umpqua pattern developed by Clarence Gordon in the 1930s. The Black Gordon is as popular a pattern today as when it was first introduced. Near endless variations exist for this fly, which is one of my favorite dark patterns.

BLACK PRINCE

HOOK: *Standard salmon or steelhead hook*
TAG: *Oval silver tinsel*
TAIL: *Red hackle fibers*
BODY: *Rear 1/3 yellow floss or wool; front 2/3 black wool*
RIB: *Oval silver tinsel*
COLLAR: *Black hen or saddle hackle*
WING: *Black hair: bear, bucktail, etc.*

A standard pattern on the North Umpqua for years, the Black Prince dates back to the late 1800s. Initially a trout fly its complete origin, along with its designer, is unknown.

GOLDEN DEMON

HOOK: *Standard salmon or steelhead hook*
TAIL: *Golden pheasant crest*
BODY: *Oval or flat or embossed gold tinsel*
COLLAR: *Orange saddle hackle*
WING: *Natural brown bucktail or red fox squirrel tail, bronze mallard is sometimes used for a featherwing*
CHEEKS: *Jungle cock (optional)*

The first Golden Demon was introduced to steelheaders by Zane Grey in the 1930s. On one of his trips to New Zealand Grey found great success with a version of this fly and brought it back for a trial run on steelhead. The Rogue and Umpqua steelhead and fishermen both took a liking to the new fly and soon it was a standard on both rivers, the Rogue especially.

GOLDEN GIRL

HOOK: *Originally, this fly was often tied on a down eyed, fairly heavy English salmon hook but this hook is no longer available. Mustad's 7970 is a good replacement or any standard salmon hook will do*
TAIL: *Yellow or orange hackle fibers*
BODY: *Flat gold tinsel*
COLLAR: *Orange saddle hackle*
WING: *A few orange polar bear hairs or bucktail, enveloped by a pair of matching golden pheasant tippets*

Roderick Haig-Brown spent much of his life fishing and living on the Campbell River. Haig-Brown was a vocal conservationist who fought to help the runs of salmon and steelhead in British Columbia. Roderick developed this fly in the 1940s with the intent of it being fished deep for winter steelhead. This fly is sometimes tied on finer wire hooks and fished for summer fish also.

Plate 4 Page 47

GREEN BUTT, LOW WATER

HOOK: *Alec Jackson Spey Hook, sizes 1 1/2-7*
TAG: *Medium flat silver tinsel*
TAIL: *Dyed red golden pheasant crest*
BODY: *Rear 1/4 fluorescent green floss; front 3/4 black floss*
RIB: *Fine oval silver tinsel over black floss only*
THROAT: *Sparse, webby hen hackle fibers*
WING: *Two matching white goose shoulder strips or two matching pairs of white hackle tips.*
CHEEKS: *Jungle cock, optional*

This low water version of the Green Butted Skunk was sent to me by Brad Burden of Portland, Oregon. Brad is one of the most gifted tiers in the Northwest and is not stingy with instruction to others.

INDIAN GIRL

HOOK: *Standard salmon iron*
TAIL: *Black hackle fibers*
BODY: *Fluorescent fire orange chenille*
RIB: *Medium oval gold tinsel*
COLLAR: *Soft black saddle hackle*
WING: *Gray squirrel tail*
HEAD: *Black*

This pattern was given to me by Joe Howell and is one of his North Umpqua patterns. The black and orange give this fly a good contrast that both fish and fishermen like.

KANDY KANE

HOOK: *Standard salmon, sizes 1-2/0*
BODY: *None*
WING: *Cerise marabou, full and long on top with a little on the underside, topped with several strands each of red Krystal Flash and silver Flashabou*
COLLAR: *Red schlappen wound full using the webby, fluffy butt end of the feather*
HEAD: *Fire orange*

George Cook originally designed this pattern for Alaskan salmon, chum, slivers, pinks and kings. It has also proven to be a good steelhead producer when a bright winter fly is required.

LADY CAROLINE

HOOK: *Standard or low water salmon iron*
TAIL: *Golden pheasant breast feather fibers*
BODY: *Blended seals fur, one part olive, two parts light brown, body should be dressed thin*
RIB: *Fine oval gold or silver tinsel*
THROAT: *Golden pheasant breast fibers*
WING: *Bronze mallard strips set low*
HEAD: *Black*

This pattern is generally tied fairly low water in style and is a good alternative to the full Spey version (See Spey chapter). I prefer using gold tinsel as opposed to silver in clear water when fish may be more timid. This sample was sent to me by Mark Kirchner.

LUNAR MIST

HOOK: *Partridge Bartleet Supreme, sizes 2-4*
TAG: *Fine oval silver tinsel*
BODY: *Bright green floss*
RIB: *Fine oval silver tinsel*
COLLAR: *White Arctic fox followed by chartreuse Arctic fox (use dubbing loop to spin and apply collar)*
HEAD: *Black*

LUNAR RUN

HOOK: *Partridge Bartleet Supreme, sizes 2-4*
TAG: *Fine oval silver tinsel*
BODY: *Flat silver tinsel*
RIB: *Fine oval silver tinsel*
COLLAR: *Black Arctic fox spun on a loop and wound as a collar*
WING: *Chartreuse Arctic fox tail*
HEAD: *Black*

Donald Storms of Oak Ridge, New Jersey developed both the Lunar Mist and the Lunar Run using Arctic fox and a spinning loop for applying a collar.

MARCH BROWN

HOOK: *Standard or low water salmon or Bartleet style Spey*
TAG: *Flat gold tinsel*
TAIL: *Strands of bronze mallard or brown partridge*
BODY: *Rear fourth yellow rabbit dubbing; front three-fourths hare's mask dubbing*
RIB: *Fine oval gold tinsel*
THROAT: *Brown partridge*
WING: *Light brown, mottled quill strips, hen pheasant tail or peacock secondary quills work well*
HEAD: *Black*

Many fishermen have begun to realize the virtues of some older, somber Atlantic salmon patterns, such as the Lady Caroline and the March Brown. Not only do these flies catch fish they also remind us of days gone by, when fish were abundant and times were simpler. The older patterns continue to thrive because of the romantic nature associated with the age old art of fly fishing.

The March Brown can be traced back to the mid-1800s as a trout pattern used in Great Britain and converted to larger versions for salmon. Rediscovered by steelhead fishermen years later, this fly is often tied low water style and fished using the greased line method originated by A.H.E. Wood, writer of *Greased Line Fishing For Salmon.*

TALUCA RABBIT MUDDLER

HOOK: *Partridge N low water hook or Mustad 9672, sizes 6-1/0*
TAIL: *Continuation of Matuka strip over body*
BODY: *Braided gold tinsel, Diamond Braid, with a gray rabbit strip tied over body matuka style*
RIB: *Medium copper wire binding down the rabbit strip*
CHEEKS: *Mottled hen hackle tips followed by a red seal fur collar, a couple of turns*
HEAD: *Natural deer hair spun and clipped to shape leaving a little for a collar*

Brad Burden designed this effective muddler variation which, with the rabbit strip, has a lot of movement. I am sure this pattern works well deep sunk or just under the surface.

McLEOD'S UGLY

HOOK: *Standard steelhead or salmon hook*
TAIL: *Red marabou-like fluff from the base of a red hackle*
BODY: *Black chenille*
HACKLE: *Grizzly palmered as a body hackle, tied in by the tip*
WING: *Black bear or other black hair*

Father and son team Ken and George McLeod developed this pattern in 1962. In faster water this fly requires a bit of weight or a high density line to get it down because of the extra resistance of the palmered hackle but this is a very buggy fly that has a lot of fish appeal.

Plate 5 Page 48

MICKEY FINN

HOOK: *Standard salmon or steelhead hook or Daiichi J101 6XL streamer hook*
BODY: *Flat or embossed silver tinsel*
WING: *One small layer of yellow bucktail and a bunch of red bucktail the same size as the first on top and another bunch yellow bucktail the size of the first two bunches combined on top of the first two*

This is an old East coast trout pattern that dates back to the early part of the 1900s. Popularized by the writings of John Alden Knight it was christened the Mickey Finn in 1936, after several years of being without a name.

Reuben Walize introduced his version of the Mickey Finn to me while he was living in Winchester, Oregon. Reuben ties his version on the 6XL streamer hook made by Daiichi that Bob Johns designed. He ties it low water style, in sizes 1 and 2, and fishes it that way summer and winter. Reuben is an Easterner himself and is quite accustomed to the Mickey Finn.

MIGRANT ORANGE

HOOK: *Standard salmon or generally, low water salmon*
TAG: *Flat copper tinsel with fluorescent orange floss covering most*
TAIL: *Fluorescent orange hackle fibers*
BODY: *Deep fluorescent orange wool*
RIB: *Flat copper tinsel*
COLLAR: *Fluorescent orange hen hackle*
WING: *Fluorescent orange hair topped with a strand of fluorescent orange yarn*

Walt Johnson developed this pattern to its present state around 1960 after years of experimenting with the orange shrimp concept. Walt has helped to give steelheading the grace it deserves with his elegant patterns. Walt fishes with midge bamboo rods and takes many fish with his delicate pieces of wood.

MUDDLER MINNOW

HOOK: *Tier's choice, standard, low water or streamer*
TAIL: *Mottled oak turkey strips*
BODY: *Flat or embossed gold tinsel, some tiers will use Diamond Braid*
WING: *Gray squirrel tail with strips of mottled turkey on each side*
HEAD AND COLLAR: *Spun deer hair to form a collar and trimmed to a bullet shaped head*

Don Gapen of Anoka, Minnesota first tied the Muddler Minnow to imitate an indigenous flat head minnow that was a good bait fish for the locals. Decades later, steelheaders have found it a useful fly fished deep or as a surface pattern. Reuben Walize fishes the North Umpqua and other rivers with the Muddler tied low water style tied on a 6XL Bob Johns streamer hook made by Daiichi in sizes 1 and 2. He fishes it in and under the surface film, twitching it through the riffles.

ONDINE

HOOK: *Alec Jackson Spey Hook, nickel*
TAIL: *Two small kingfisher feathers, back to back*
TAG: *Fine oval silver tinsel and black floss, ahead of the tail*
BUTT: *Black ostrich, very small*
BODY: *Rear half black silk floss; front half black Angora goat*
RIB: *Bright blue floss with fine oval silver tinsel on each side, over the rear half only*
COLLAR: *Guinea hen dyed kingfisher blue, followed by a gray Spey hackle, long, to the bend of hook*
HEAD: *Black*

Mark Kirchner came up with this soft hackle pattern for steelhead. A dark pattern like this would make a great low water summer pattern. Mark resides in Newport Beach, California and is a photographer by trade, he did the color fly plates for this book.

PAINT BRUSH

HOOK: *Mustad 7970, sizes 1-4*
BODY: *Flat gold tinsel*
HACKLE: *Deep reddish-orange palmered over body, tied in by the tip*
COLLAR: *Purple followed by bright turquoise saddle hackle*
HEAD: *Claret or red*

Bill McMillan is an advocate of floating fly lines for winter fish and has developed several patterns specifically for his method of fishing, the Paint Brush is one of them. The hackles should be tapered slightly from back to front with the purple being a little longer than the orange and the blue a little longer than the purple. Bill suggests that the fly be fished on a dead drift casting far enough upstream to allow the fly to reach the desired depth.

PAYOFF

HOOK: *Standard salmon hook, sizes 1-2/0*
BODY: *None*
WING: *Very deep purple marabou fairly thick and long with a small bunch under the hook topped with a few strands each of red Krystal Flash and purple Flashabou*
COLLAR: *Red schlappen wound full using the webby, fluffy butt end of the feather*
HEAD: *Fire orange*

The Sauk, Skagit and Skykomish rivers are proven waters for the Payoff, one of George Cook's patterns. George says that this fly has a "big time winter run color scheme".

POLAR BUTT BLACK BEAR, GREEN

HOOK: *Bartleet or standard salmon*
TAG: *Fine oval silver tinsel and fluorescent green floss*
TAIL: *Chartreuse polar bear hair*
BODY: *Rear 2/3 black leech yarn; front 1/3 black schlappen packed tight, tie in the schlappen by the tip and use the whole feather including the fluff*
RIB: *Medium oval silver tinsel over the yarn only*
WING: *Black bear*
COLLAR: *Black schlappen*
CHEEKS: *Jungle cock*

Joe Rossano used the Green Butt Black Bear, an Atlantic salmon hairwing, as the basis for this pattern. Joe has also had good luck with a red version, tag and tail, taking several fish over the 40 inch mark on the Bulkey.

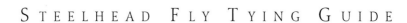

POLAR SHRIMP

HOOK: *Tiers choice, standard or low water*
TAG: *Flat gold tinsel*
TAIL: *Red hackle fibers*
BODY: *Fluorescent orange chenille*
COLLAR: *Orange saddle hackle*
WING: *White hair, bucktail, polar bear, Arctic fox, etc.*
HEAD: *Black, red or orange*

The Polar Shrimp has been a popular pattern for over 50 years, dating back to the mid-1930s. Well-known on the Eel River, this fly has many fans throughout the Northwest. Its originator may have been an employee of Shoff's Tackle in Kent, Washington or possibly Clarence Shoff himself. The original Polar Shrimp was tied with polar bear for the wing, the only difference between it and the Orange Shrimp. Today the wing material does not constitute a change in name, with many different wing materials being used.

PURPLE FLASH

HOOK: *Standard salmon hook*
TAG: *Flat gold tinsel*
TAIL: *Red hackle fibers*
BODY: *Purple braided Mylar; Diamond Braid, Poly Flash, etc.*
COLLAR: *Deep purple saddle or hen hackle*
WING: *Red fox squirrel tail*
CHEEKS: *Jungle cock*
HEAD: *Black*

Whenever a new material hits the market Joe Howell is one of the first to find a use for it. Joe's creativity is part of what makes him a top-notch tier, that and pure skill.

Plate 6 Page 49

PURPLE PERIL

HOOK: *Tiers choice, standard hook*
TAG: *Flat silver tinsel*
TAIL: *Purple hackle fibers*
BODY: *Purple floss, wool or chenille*
RIB: *Flat or oval silver tinsel*
COLLAR: *Purple saddle hackle*
WING: *Mottled deer body hair, brown bucktail or red fox squirrel tail*

The first dressing for this fly I remember seeing was tied with floss for the body and deer hair for the wing. Today most Purple Perils I see have chenille for the body and squirrel for the wing. Ken McLeod's fly has seen some subtle changes since its introduction in the late 1930s. Purple is a wonderful color for most light conditions as it appears dark, yet under low light it retains its color well because it is at the end of the color spectrum.

PURPLE PERIL, LOW WATER

HOOK: *Alec Jackson Spey Hook, sizes 1 1/2-7*
TAG: *Medium flat silver tinsel*
TAIL: *Dyed purple golden pheasant crest*
BODY: *Purple floss, dressed thin*
RIB: *Fine oval silver tinsel*
THROAT: *Sparse, webby hen hackle fibers dyed purple*
WING: *Bronze mallard strips set low over the body*

Low water Purple Perils are not uncommon and this version is Brad Burden's. I often use purple seal fur for the body, dressed very thin, instead of floss but other than that this is the dressing I have fished for a long time.

PURPLE RAT, WINTER DRESS

HOOK: *Bartleet or standard salmon hook*
THREAD: *Orange*
TAG: *Fine oval silver tinsel*
TAIL: *Golden pheasant breast feather*
BODY: *Rear 2/3 purple leech yarn; front 1/3 purple schlappen wound tight, tie in the feather by the tip and use the whole feather including the fluff*
RIB: *Fine oval silver tinsel over the yarn only*
WING: *Gray fox*
COLLAR: *Grizzly hen hackle*
CHEEKS: *Jungle cock*
HEAD: *Orange*

This is Joe Rosanno's takeoff on the Rat series made famous by Atlantic salmon fishermen. This is a fuller version and gives a much larger profile for high winter conditions.

RAINBOW SERIES

This is a series of flies that Mel Simpson of Freemont, California has developed using Edward L. Haas' method of wing mounting. Mel uses the same basic design on all of his Rainbow flies making some changes for featherwings and his Spey flies, (See Spey chapter). Mel sent me a full set of his hairwing flies and a sample each of his featherwing and Spey flies. The rainbow effect is achieved by using colored felt-tipped waterproof markers over the embossed tinsel bodies and coating them with head cement.

Mel has a great respect for the late Edward L. Haas and uses his wing mounting style on his hairwing flies. By slightly spreading open the eye on looped eye hooks and trapping the wing hairs between the loop you can create a nearly indestructible wing. The wing is tied in first with the tips pointing forward and the butts are tied down as an underbody. After the tail, body, rib and hackle are applied the wing is then folded back and tied down. This gives the potential for a small head and a very rugged fly.

RAINBOW HAIRWING

HOOK: *Daiichi #J141*
THREAD: *8/0 white on all color flies*
TAG: *Two turns of medium flat oval silver tinsel*
TAIL: *15 hairs of dyed squirrel tail*
UNDERBODY: *Taper towards shoulder with white floss*
BODY: *Medium embossed French tinsel dyed with waterproof marker coated with head cement (Mel uses MARKS-A-LOT or El-Marko brand markers and blends it lighter to darker from back to front leaving a short space of silver near the tail) Double wrap the body from shoulder to tail and back*
RIB: *Medium flat oval silver tinsel, applied after body dries, it is a continuation of the tag. This should cock the tail up slightly*
COLLAR: *Dyed neck hackle, 3 1/2 turns*
WING: *20 dyed or natural white polar bear hairs topped with 15 dyed squirrel tail hairs, Ed Haas style*
CHEEKS: *Jungle cock*
HEAD: *Dyed with marker to match color of the fly*

The colors on Mel's flies are consistent with each fly; dyed red squirrel, dyed red polar bear, red hackle and red marker. Colors, of course, are based on whatever color of markers can be found. Mel chooses his hairwing flies for deep sunk faster water.

RAINBOW FEATHERWING

HOOK: Partridge #SEB
THREAD: 8/0 white
TAG: Two turns of medium flat oval silver tinsel
BODY: Medium embossed silver tinsel dyed with waterproof marker, as on hairwing version, and coated with head cement
RIB: Medium flat oval silver tinsel, applied after body dries, this is a continuation of tag
COLLAR: Dyed neck hackle, 3 1/2 turns, mallard flank for throat
WING: Bronze mallard strips set low
HEAD: Dyed with same felt marker as body

Mel recommends his down eyed featherwings for subsurface greased line fishing.

RED ABBEY, WINTER DRESS

HOOK: Bartleet or standard salmon
THREAD: Black
TAG: Fine oval silver tinsel
TAIL: Red polar bear
BODY: Rear 2/3 red leech yarn; front 1/3 red schlappen wound tight, tie in the feather by the tip and use the whole feather, including the fluff
RIB: Embossed silver tinsel over the yarn only
WING: Brown bear
COLLAR: Brown hen hackle
CHEEKS: Jungle cock

Joe Rossano's eastern influence led him to using the Atlantic salmon hairwing, Red Abbey, for the basis of his red winter pattern.

Plate 7 Page 50

RED ANT

HOOK: Standard or low water salmon or steelhead hook, on the Rogue River small doubles are commonly used
TAG: Fine oval silver tinsel
TAIL: Red hackle fibers
BUTT: Peacock herl
BODY: Red floss or wool
COLLAR: Furnace hackle
WING: Red fox squirrel tail

Mike Kennedy's Red Ant is a fine summer pattern which gained its popularity on the Rogue but is effective in any low water situation.

RED ANT, FEATHERWING LOW WATER (Burden)

HOOK: Alec Jackson Spey Hook, sizes 1 1/2-7
TAG: Medium Flat silver tinsel
TAIL: Dyed red golden pheasant crest
BUTT: Peacock herl
BODY: Red floss
RIB: Fine oval silver tinsel
THROAT: Sparse, webby brown hen hackle fibers
WING: Bronze mallard, set low over the body

Brad Burden's dressing for the Rogue River standard varies slightly from the original but this example shows some diversity in material selection, in the wing and the rib. Brad, along with many others, feels that featherwings give more movement and life to an already good pattern.

RICK'S REVENGE

HOOK: Alec Jackson Spey Hook, sizes 3-7, nickel or gold
TAIL: Fluorescent pink floss
BODY: Rear half fluorescent pink floss; front half purple seal. Veil at the joint with a strand or two of fluorescent pink floss
RIB: Fine oval gold tinsel over seal only
WING: White polar bear topped with a few strands of purple polar bear
COLLAR: Purple hen hackle
HEAD: Claret

Rick's Revenge is one of the few non Spey patterns that John Shewey developed. An exceptionally bright fly, it works well in both summer and winter.

ROYAL COACHMAN

HOOK: Tiers choice, standard or low water
TAG: Flat gold tinsel
TAIL: Golden pheasant tippet fibers
BODY: Rear fourth peacock herl; middle half red floss; front fourth peacock herl
COLLAR: Dyed reddish-brown hackle, Coachman brown
WING: White hair, bucktail, polar bear, etc. or white goose shoulder strips
CHEEKS: Jungle cock, optional
HEAD: Black or red

The royal family, during much of the 1800s, had Tom Bosworth as its coachman. Tom was also a fisherman and fly tier. His introduction of the Coachman made him semi-famous, the addition of golden pheasant tippet for the tail and the red floss center-joint made the Royal Coachman. This the most recognized fly in America and after all these years it still catches fish.

The featherwing version shown is part of Joe Rossano's American Low Water series. This low water dressing was inspired by Ray Bergman's wet flies in his classic book, Trout.

ROYAL COACHMAN (Kirchner)

HOOK: Alec Jackson Spey Hook, nickel
TAG: Fine oval silver tinsel, ahead of the tail
TAIL: One pair of very small golden pheasant tippets
BUTT: Peacock herl
BODY: Rear half red silk floss; front half peacock herl, it's a good idea to form the peacock herl into a chenille with fine oval gold tinsel, Alec Jackson style
COLLAR: Teal flank, long
WING: Two sections of white goose shoulder set low
HEAD: Red, small

This version of an old standard was sent to me by Mark Kirchner of Newport Beach, California. Along with being a very good fly tier, Mark is a professional photographer who uses his extra film photographing his intricate salmon and steelhead flies.

RUSTY RAT

HOOK: Standard or low water salmon
TAG: Fine oval gold tinsel
TAIL: Peacock sword fibers
BODY: Rear half deep golden yellow floss; front half peacock herl. Veil above at the center with one strand of golden yellow floss over rear half of body
RIB: Fine oval gold tinsel
WING: Gray fox guard hairs
CHEEKS: Jungle cock, optional
COLLAR: Grizzly hen
HEAD: Red

Another Atlantic salmon hairwing pattern that migrated west and has been proven worthy on the Pacific steelhead as well. Roy Angus Thompson developed the first Rat flies with several variations being developed by others. The Rusty Rat is one of them. It was developed by J. C. "Clovie" Arseneault.

S.S.S.

HOOK: *Standard salmon or low water salmon hook*
TAG: *Flat tinsel*
TAIL: *Dyed squirrel tail to match the fly color*
BODY: *Seal fur or Angora goat dyed to match the fly color*
RIB: *Fine oval tinsel*
COLLAR: *Dyed saddle hackle to match the rest of the fly*
WING: *Dyed squirrel tail to match the fly*
HEAD: *Thread to match the fly*

Chuck Gilbert from Portland, Oregon has one of the greatest jobs. He travels the Northwest with his fly rod in tow, showing off the newest and best in fly fishing gear, stopping when and where the fishing might be good. He says the life fits. Chuck developed the S.S.S. (Steelhead, Seal and Squirrel) with the idea of using the same color throughout the fly. He ties them in blue, black, purple, green, yellow, tan, red, wine, white and brown. He uses silver tinsel in blue tones and gold with brown tones.

SACRAMENTO RIVER COACHMAN

HOOK: *Alec Jackson Spey Hook*
TAG: *Flat silver tinsel*
TAIL: *Golden pheasant tippet fibers*
BODY: *Peacock herl with center joint of golden yellow floss, Royal Coachman style*
RIB: *Fine gold tinsel or wire, counter wrapped from tail*
COLLAR: *Yellow golden pheasant rump feather*
WING: *Tan goose shoulder strips set low*
CHEEKS: *Jungle cock*
TOPPING: *Two golden pheasant crests*

David Burns of McCall, Idaho sent his Coachman variation which is a good low, clear water fly.

SALMON RIVER PURPLE SKUNK

HOOK: *Standard salmon, TMC 7999 etc.*
TAG: *Extra fine oval silver tinsel*
TAIL: *Golden pheasant crest*
BUTT: *Fluorescent green chenille or wool*
BODY: *Bright violet floss*
RIB: *Small oval silver tinsel*
COLLAR: *Soft green-black hen or saddle hackle*
WING: *Badger, tied in forward under body and pulled back over hackle, Ed Haas style*
TOPPING: *Peacock sword*

David Burns of McCall, Idaho designed this pattern and has good success on his home river, the South Fork of the Salmon.

Plate 8 Page 51

SHEDLOCK SPIDERS
BLACK SPIDER

HOOK: *Low water salmon, Partridge N*
THREAD: *Fluorescent green*
TAG: *Fine oval silver tinsel*
BODY: *Black seal or substitute*
COLLAR: *Teal*
HEAD: *Fluorescent green*

BROWN SPIDER

HOOK: *Low water salmon, Partridge N*
THREAD: *Yellow*
TAG: *Fine oval gold tinsel*
BODY: *Brown seal or substitute*
COLLAR: *Lemon woodduck*
HEAD: *Yellow*

DNA SPIDER

HOOK: *Low water salmon, Partridge N*
THREAD: *Orange*
TAG: *Fine oval silver tinsel*
BODY: *Orange and red mixed seal fur, thin*
COLLAR: *Mallard*
HEAD: *Orange*

Since 1977 this Spider series has taken sea-run fish on both coasts. The DNA was first developed by Joseph Shedlock. During the time that Joe Rossano and Joseph Shedlock fished together they developed the other two patterns. They are simple yet effective in extreme low water conditions.

SILVER ANT

HOOK: *Standard or low water salmon or steelhead hook*
TAIL: *Red hackle fibers*
BUTT: *Black chenille or ostrich herl*
BODY: *Oval or flat embossed silver tinsel*
COLLAR: *Black saddle hackle*
WING: *White calftail or Arctic fox tail*
CHEEKS: *Jungle cock, optional*

Ike Tower of Coos Bay, Oregon has been most often credited with the development of this Rogue River pattern. Fished on the Rogue it is tied on small hooks, often doubles, and the wing is tied upright and divided. The Silver Ant also makes a good low water pattern tied in a streamlined dressing.

SILVER DEMON

HOOK: *Standard salmon or steelhead hook*
TAG: *Oval silver tinsel*
TAIL: *Orange hackle fibers*
BODY: *Flat silver tinsel*
COLLAR: *Full, stiff orange saddle hackle*
WING: *Badger, gray fox or ground squirrel*
CHEEKS: *Jungle cock (optional)*
HEAD: *Black*

This is Jim Pray's standard pattern developed for the Eel and other northern California rivers. Jim Pray's original version used oval silver tinsel for the body and the gray fox guard hairwing is my preference.

SILVER HILTON

HOOK: *Standard salmon or steelhead hook*
TAIL: *Mallard flank fibers*
BODY: *Black chenille*
RIB: *Oval or flat silver tinsel*
WING: *Two grizzly hackle tips curving outward*
COLLAR: *Grizzly hackle tied somewhat full, softer hackle is generally preferred*

Introduced after World War II in northern California, the Silver Hilton is a popular pattern in the Northwest for summer fish. The originator is all but forgotten but his dressing has bred many variations over the years.

SKUNK, STANDARD

HOOK: *Tier's choice*
TAIL: *Red hackle fibers*
BODY: *Black chenille*
RIB: *Silver tinsel*
COLLAR: *Black hackle*
WING: *White hair, polar bear, bucktail, calftail, etc.*

This fly, and versions of it, is without a doubt the most popular steelhead fly. It has lead to numerous spinoffs with and without the Skunk name. The originator of the Skunk is debatable, Wes Drain has been mentioned along with Mildred Krogel and others as possible designers of this fly. The time frame of the 1930's or 1940's has often been given for its introduction.

SKUNK, COASTAL (Jackson)

HOOK: Alec Jackson Spey Hook or tiers choice depending on fishing conditions
TAIL: Stiff, red hackle fibers
BODY: Dressed rather thin with a chenille made with peacock herl or fine ostrich or both twisted with a strand of fine, oval silver tinsel
COLLAR: Stiff hen hackle, black. Alec refers to this as "cocky" hen
WING: White hair, Alec prefers polar bear mask. Don't dress the wing very full

Alec Jackson is a serious and astute angler who has learned over the years that a large variety of patterns is not as important as having a fly tied in the right manner for a fishing situation. By tying a Skunk in several styles he is able to fish most fishing situations with confidence. He may fish his Skunks as large as 3/0 or as small as he finds appropriate.

SKUNK, INLAND (Jackson)

HOOK: Alec Jackson Spey Hook
TAIL: Red hackle fibers
BODY: Plump black ostrich herl chenille, sometimes Alec uses peacock herl chenille for the rear third of the body
COLLAR: Stiff black cocks hackle
WING: Fine, sparse polar bear hair

A plumper, more visible version for steelhead that have been in fresh water for some time. The steelhead's vision may begin to fail as a result of the breakdown in the fish's body due to the long trip and the dying process that hits many traveling steelhead.

SKUNK (Kirchner, Featherwing)

HOOK: Alec Jackson Spey Hook, nickel
TAG: Fine oval silver tinsel, applied after the tail, more like a butt
TAIL: Scarlet silk floss, four turns
BODY: Rear half black floss; front half small black feathers tied in layers, as in the "Chatterer", an old Atlantic salmon pattern
RIB: Fine oval silver tinsel over the floss section only
COLLAR: Blue eared pheasant dyed black, black heron substitute
WING: Lady Amherst pheasant tail sections set fairly low
HEAD: Black, small

Mark Kirchner of Newport Beach, California uses his many skills as a full-dressed Atlantic salmon fly tier when designing a new steelhead fly or a new version of an old standard like the Skunk. Even though Mark lives a ways from any steelhead waters he has a tremendous grasp on use of materials for a certain application. This is one of the most mobile and graceful versions of a Skunk this side of a full-fledged Spey fly. Feathers from the neck of a Chinese pheasant dyed black work well for the body on this fly.

Plate 9 Page 52

SPADE (Arnold)

HOOK: Tier's choice, standard or low water
TAIL: Natural deer hair
BODY: Black chenille
COLLAR: Grizzly

This is the original Spade that Bob Arnold introduced to the North Fork of the Stillaguamish River in the 1960s. Many variations have evolved, the most famous are the Spade series that Alec Jackson developed.

SPADE, PLAIN (Jackson)

HOOK: Alec Jackson Spey Hook
TAIL: Very fine deer hair, dik dik, impala etc.
BODY: Peacock herl twisted with fine oval tinsel to form a chenille and wound starting above the point of the hook
COLLAR: Grizzly

Alec Jackson has helped bring grace to steelhead fly fishing, partly because of his classic Alec Jackson Spey Hook and also because of his attitude and willingness to help and demonstrate. His hooks are sought after and not always easily obtainable but are worth the search. His teachings are informative and invaluable to the discriminating tier.

This version of the basic Spade is dressed in several different degrees of "portliness". Alec will dress his patterns differently for various fishing situations. Fatter flies for inland situations, thinner flies for coastal areas. Alec feels that the further inland you are, the larger the silhouette. The natural break down of the fish's body affects its sight, Alec feels, and the larger fly is more effective.

SPADE, FANCY (Jackson)

HOOK: Alec Jackson Spey Hook
TAIL: Very fine deer hair or impala
BODY: Rear third or half peacock herl chenille; balance black ostrich herl twisted into a chenille with fine tinsel
COLLAR: Grizzly

SPADE, CLARET GUINEA (Jackson)

HOOK: Alec Jackson Spey Hook
TAIL: Very fine deer body hair or impala, the hair around the muzzle of a deer mask or the hocks of a deer work well
BUTT: Hot red fuzzy yarn or red ostrich herl. This is sometimes tied as a butt after the tail or as a tag, very short under the tail
BODY: Black ostrich wound with fine oval silver tinsel to form a chenille, use large ostrich and several strands (4-10) depending on desired fullness of body
COLLAR: Fairly stiff grizzly followed by longer guinea dyed claret-red

This is one of Alec Jackson's adaptations of the Spade. Alec is one of steelheading's most innovative fly tiers with his ostrich chenille and seal dubbing techniques. Today's fly tier has Alec to thank for many innovative tying methods. Changing the butt and guinea collar to yellow transform this fly into a Yellow Guinea Spade.

SPADE, YELLOW GUINEA (Jackson)

HOOK: Alec Jackson Spey Hook
TAIL: Very fine deer or impala
BUTT: Yellow fuzzy yarn or yellow ostrich herl, sometimes the yellow yarn is tied under the tail as a tag
COLLAR: Fairly stiff grizzly followed by longer yellow guinea

SPADE, PURPLE (Jackson)

HOOK: Alec Jackson Spey Hook
TAIL: Very fine deer or impala
BODY: Rear half or two thirds purple peacock herl chenille; balance purple ostrich herl chenille
COLLAR: Stiff grizzly hen or soft rooster, sometimes followed by purple guinea hen

SPADE, WHAKA BLONDE (Jackson)

HOOK: Alec Jackson Spey Hook
TAIL: Purple hackle fibers
BODY: Purple ostrich, 6-8 strands twisted with fine oval silver tinsel to form a chenille rope. Occasionally Alec ties it with the rear portion of the body being purple peacock herl chenille
COLLAR: Purple hen hackle

Alec's all purple Spade has become a popular alternative to the original black Spade. Generally, Alec ties this fly "plump", along the "inland" lines.

SPADE, JACOB'S COAT (Jackson)

HOOK: *Alec Jackson Spey Hook*
TAIL: *Very fine deer or impala*
BODY: *One strand each of whatever color peacock and ostrich herl is available or on the bench at the time, twisted with fine tinsel into a chenille*
COLLAR: *Whatever looks good with what you use for the body*

SPRUCE

HOOK: *Standard or low water salmon hook*
TAIL: *Peacock sword fibers, five to seven*
BODY: *Rear 1/3 red floss; balance peacock herl*
WING: *Two badger hackle tips curved outward*
COLLAR: *Badger hackle*

During the 1930s, the Spruce was designed as a sea-run cutthroat pattern for use in Seaside, Oregon. My research on this fly indicates that a gentleman known as Godfrey is generally given credit for the development of the Spruce.

The Spruce makes an outstanding summer fly when the water is clear. Another alternative is to dress the fly with furnace hackle for the wings and collar, thus creating the Dark Spruce.

Plate 10 Page 53

STEELHEAD BEAR, DARK BLACK BEAR

HOOK: *Low water salmon or Alec Jackson Spey Hook*
TAG: *Flat gold tinsel*
TAIL: *Teal flank*
BODY: *Dark black bear fur dubbing*
THROAT: *Black hen hackle*
WING: *Dyed black turkey strips*
HEAD: *Black*

STEELHEAD BEAR, DARK GRIZZLY

This pattern is the same as the previous "Bear" with the exception of the body which is dubbed from brown bear fur. Joe Rossano has developed the Steelhead Bear series as a low, clear water set of patterns. Joe ties these flies low water in proportion and on small hooks. This series consists of several other patterns, all using bear fur as the body with various color combinations.

STEELHEAD CANDY

This series of flies was originated by Bill Black of Roseburg, Oregon. Bill, and his partner Ken Ferguson, recently established Spirit River Inc., a wholesale fly and material business. They have developed and marketed new materials and have incorporated some of them in this set of flies.

Bill says of these flies, "This entire series gets down where the steelhead take. These flies are fast to tie, durable and the rabbit wing creates a fair amount of movement". The Lite Brite that Bill mentions is a new, very thin, shredded Mylar product that Spirit River distributes.

BLACK'S OLD GRIZZLY

HOOK: *Daiichi 2441, Tiemco 7999 or standard salmon, sizes 2/0-6*
THREAD: *Black 6/0*
TAG: *Flat gold tinsel*
BODY: *Ocean Blue colored Lite Brite Mylar, dubbed and picked out*
RIB: *Flat gold tinsel*
WING: *Natural grizzly colored, 1/8" wide zonker rabbit strip*
COLLAR: *Soft grizzly saddle hackle, substitute black*
EYES: *Gold colored Dazl-Eyes*
HEAD: *Dubbed Lite Brite Mylar around eyes, same color as body*

BLACK'S BUNNY SKUNK

HOOK: *Tiemco 7999, Daiichi 2441 or standard salmon, sizes 2/0-6*
THREAD: *Black 6/0*
TAG: *Flat silver tinsel*
TAIL: *None*
BUTT: *Black ostrich herl*
BODY: *Fire Fox Peacock colored Lite Brite Mylar, shredded and dubbed and picked out*
RIB: *Flat silver tinsel*
WING: *White 1/8" wide rabbit strip (Zonker strip)*
COLLAR: *Black saddle hackle*
EYES: *Nickel-plated Dazl-Eyes, solid brass eyes*
HEAD: *Dubbed Lite Brite Mylar, same color as body, around eyes*

BLACK'S SOFT CANDY CAIN

HOOK: *Daiichi 2441, Tiemco 7999 or standard salmon, sizes 2/0-6*
THREAD: *Red or white 6/0*
TAG: *Flat gold tinsel*
BUTT: *Red ostrich herl, optional*
BODY: *Salmon pink colored Lite Brite Mylar, dubbed and picked out*
RIB: *Flat gold tinsel*
WING: *White, 1/8" wide zonker rabbit strip*
COLLAR: *Soft red saddle hackle*
EYES: *Gold colored Dazl-Eyes*
HEAD: *Dubbed Lite Brite Mylar around eyes, same color as body*

BLACK'S SOFT SWIMMING SUNRISE

HOOK: *Daiichi 2441, Tiemco 7999 or standard salmon, sizes 2/0-6*
THREAD: *Red 6/0*
TAG: *Flat gold tinsel*
BUTT: *Red ostrich herl, optional*
BODY: *Copper colored Lite Brite Mylar, dubbed and picked out, substitute hot yellow*
RIB: *Flat gold tinsel*
WING: *Hot Yellow, 1/8" wide Zonker rabbit strip*
COLLAR: *Soft red saddle hackle*
EYES: *Gold colored Dazl-Eyes*
HEAD: *Lite Brite Mylar dubbed around eyes, same color as body*

BLACK'S SWIMMING SUN STREAK

HOOK: *Daiichi 2441, Tiemco 7999 or standard salmon, sizes 2/0-6*
THREAD: *White 6/0*
TAG: *Flat gold tinsel*
BUTT: *White or orange ostrich herl, optional*
BODY: *Polar Pearl colored Lite Brite Mylar, dubbed and picked out*
RIB: *Flat gold tinsel*
WING: *Dyed hot orange, 1/8" wide Zonker rabbit strip*
COLLAR: *Soft, white saddle hackle ahead of wing*
EYES: *Brass colored Dazl-Eyes*
HEAD: *Lite Brite Mylar dubbed around eyes, same color as body*

BUMBLE BEE BUNNY

HOOK: *Daiichi 2441 or Tiemco 7999, sizes 2/0-6*
TAG: *Flat gold tinsel*
BUTT: *Black ostrich herl*
BODY: *Hot yellow Lite Brite shredded Mylar dubbed and picked out*
RIB: *Flat gold tinsel*
COLLAR: *Soft black saddle hackle*
WING: *Black, 1/8" rabbit zonker strip*
EYES: *Brass Dazl Eyes*
HEAD: *Hot yellow Lite Brite dubbed around eyes*

FLOOZIE

HOOK: *Daiichi 2441 or Tiemco 7999, sizes 2/0-6*
TAG: *Flat silver tinsel*
BUTT: *Black ostrich herl*
BODY: *Burgundy Lite Brite shredded Mylar, dubbed and picked out*
RIB: *Flat silver tinsel*
COLLAR: *Black saddle hackle*
WING: *Hot pink, 1/8" rabbit zonker strip*
EYES: *Nickel plated Dazl-eyes*
HEAD: *Burgundy Lite Brite, dubbed around the eyes*

MEGAN BLACK'S DELIGHT

HOOK: Daiichi 2441, TMC 7999, sizes 2/0-6
TAG: Flat gold tinsel
BUTT: Black ostrich herl
BODY: Purple Haze Lite Brite Mylar dubbed and picked out
RIB: Flat gold tinsel
COLLAR: Soft black saddle hackle
WING: 1/8" wide purple rabbit zonker strip
EYES: Brass Dazl-Eyes
HEAD: Lite Brite Mylar dubbed around eyes, same color as body

Plate 11 Page 54

STRIP WINGS (HUNT)

This series of flies was the idea of Greg Scot Hunt of Redmond, Washington. Based on the simple strip wing flies of Atlantic salmon lore, these flies are productive summer patterns with inherent beauty. These patterns are of the same structural lines and all use an eye made of a braided Dacron loop. The Dacron eye gives natural movement to the fly and Greg uses it on most of his fishing flies. Greg modifies an Alec Jackson Spey Hook by converting it to a blind eyed hook in sizes 3-7. In T. E. Pryce-Tannatt's, *How to Dress Salmon Flies*, the description of this wing would be to set it "upright", a term that many trout anglers would interpret as being completely vertical as on a dry fly.

I have included most of Greg's strip wing patterns in one section because of the way they are tied and the fact that the color scheme is all that separates them, with the exception of his Skunk. This will be easier than if they were scattered throughout this chapter.

GOLD AND RED

TAG: Fine oval silver tinsel
TAIL: Golden pheasant crest
BODY: Rear half flat gold tinsel; front half medium red floss
RIB: Fine oval silver tinsel
COLLAR: Dyed red hen hackle or schlappen
WING: Mottled turkey tail strips
CHEEKS: Jungle cock
HEAD: Black

ORANGE AND BLACK

THREAD: Yellow 6/0
TAG: Fine oval silver tinsel
TAIL: Golden pheasant crest
BODY: Rear half orange floss; front half black floss
RIB: Fine oval silver tinsel
COLLAR: Dyed black hen hackle or schlappen
WING: Mottled turkey tail strips
CHEEKS: Jungle cock
HEAD: Black

ORANGE AND CLARET

TAG: Fine oval silver tinsel
TAIL: Golden pheasant crest
BODY: Rear half orange floss; front half claret floss
RIB: Fine oval silver tinsel
COLLAR: Dyed claret hen hackle or schlappen
WING: Mottled turkey tail strips
CHEEKS: Jungle cock
HEAD: Black

SILVER AND BLUE

THREAD: Black 6/0
TAG: Fine oval silver tinsel
TAIL: Golden pheasant crest
BODY: Rear half flat silver tinsel; front half medium blue floss
RIB: Fine oval silver tinsel
COLLAR: Dyed light blue hen hackle or schlappen
WING: Mottled turkey tail strips
CHEEKS: Jungle cock
HEAD: Black

SKUNK

HOOK: Alec Jackson Spey Hook, modified blind eye
EYE: 20lb braided Dacron loop
THREAD: Black 6/0
TAG: Fine oval silver tinsel
TAIL: Golden pheasant crest
BODY: Rear half bright green floss; front half black floss
RIB: Fine oval silver tinsel
COLLAR: Dyed black hen hackle or schlappen
WING: Mottled turkey tail strips
CHEEKS: Jungle cock
HEAD: Black

YELLOW AND VIOLET

THREAD: Yellow 6/0
TAG: Fine oval silver tinsel
TAIL: Golden pheasant crest
BODY: Rear half yellow floss; front half violet floss
RIB: Fine oval silver tinsel
COLLAR: Dyed violet hen hackle or schlappen
WING: Mottled turkey tail strips
CHEEKS: Jungle cock
HEAD: Black

STEELHEAD WOOLHEAD

HOOK: Partridge CS17, Ken Baker steamer hook, size 1
THREAD: Black 6/0
BODY: Olive rabbit strip wound over hook
RIB: Wide pearl Mylar
WING: Purple rabbit strip, tied down at the tail
GILLS: Red rabbit dubbing, one turn as a collar
SIDES: Purple ringneck pheasant rump feathers, one on each side, concave side out. These represent pectoral fins
HEAD: Rams wool spun on as deer hair on a muddler, purple on top and olive on bottom

Mike Kinney of Oso, Washington designed this deep sunk sculpin type imitation. Mike spends his time on the banks of the Skagit system.

STEELIE BUGGER

HOOK: Standard salmon or steelhead hook, heavy wired hooks work best to help get the fly down I prefer the Daiichi J141 Bob Johns Winter Run
TAIL: Fine marabou blood quill and a few strands of blending Krystal Flash or Flashabou
BODY: Chenille
HACKLE: Matching color saddle hackle palmered over body with a couple of turns taken at the shoulder
RIB: Oval silver tinsel counter wound across the hackle
EYES: Large bead-chain or lead eyes depending on the depth of water

Basically a glorified Woolly Bugger, this fly is a productive pattern summer or winter. Colors are endless but black and purple are most popular with brown and orange combinations working well in summer when crayfish are out and about. There are many variations of the Woolly Bugger used for steelhead. This is just one of them.

SUMMER TWILIGHT

HOOK: Low water or Bartleet style Spey hook, I prefer the Alec Jackson Spey Hook in a gold finish
TAG: Fine oval gold tinsel
BODY: Rear third red floss; balance purple seal or substitute
COLLAR: Long, soft lavender hackle followed by a dyed red golden pheasant rump feather
WING: Married strips of red and lavender goose shoulder, alternating red, lavender, red, etc.
CHEEKS: Jungle cock
HEAD: Red

The red and purple tones of this fly make it a good evening pattern. I developed it for the last bit of light on summer evenings.

Plate 12 Page 55

THE THIEF IS GREATER THAN HIS LOOT

HOOK: *Alec Jackson Spey Hook, nickel*
TAG: *Fine oval gold tinsel and hot pink floss*
BODY: *Rear third black floss butted with small purple hackle; balance is black floss, very thin*
RIB: *Purple floss with fine oval gold tinsel on both sides of the floss over the rear third only*
THROAT: *Peacock swords*
SIDES: *Small, gray peacock pheasant body feathers, extending to the butted hackle, covering the front two thirds of the body*
HACKLE: *Gray heron substitute*
HEAD: *Small black*

Mark Kirchner devised this soft hackle style summer pattern. The soft hackle style of steelhead fly is not encountered often and can be very effective on summer fish. A large jungle cock feather cut short could be substituted for the hard-to-find peacock pheasant.

UMPQUA SPECIAL

HOOK: *Standard salmon or steelhead*
TAIL: *White hackle fibers or hair*
BODY: *Rear third yellow floss or wool; balance red wool or chenille*
RIB: *Medium oval silver tinsel*
WING: *White hair; bucktail, calftail etc. with a small bunch of red hair or strip of red goose on each side*
COLLAR: *Brown saddle hackle, fairly full, wound after the wing is applied*
CHEEKS: *Jungle cock, the jungle cock makes it "special", otherwise it is just called the Umpqua*

The Umpqua Special at first glance seems to be, and probably is, a combination of several flies of the early 1900s. Traces of the Van Luven, Parmachene Belle and Royal Coachman are apparent. Vic O'Byrne is most often given credit for this fly's design in the mid-1930s, during the fish camp boom on the North Umpqua River. Years ago, *Field and Stream* magazine ran a pattern listing for this fly and received twenty dressings "correcting their error", no two were alike. The similarities between this dressing and the Rogue River Special are amazing.

UNDERTAKER

HOOK: *Standard or low water salmon iron*
TAG: *In thirds, starting with fine oval or flat gold tinsel followed by fluorescent green floss followed by fluorescent red/orange floss. I prefer to use flat gold and use it as an underwrap for the floss to help retain the brilliance*
BODY: *Peacock herl*
RIB: *fine oval gold tinsel*
COLLAR: *Natural or dyed black hen hackle*
WING: *Black bear or other fine black hair*
CHEEKS: *Jungle cock, optional*

This is an Atlantic salmon pattern developed by Warren Duncan of Saint John, New Brunswick in 1979. This is one of the more popular Atlantic salmon/steelhead flies in some areas and a good dark pattern.

VOLCANO

HOOK: *Standard salmon hook, sizes 1-2/0*
BODY: *None*
WING: *Tied above and below, orange marabou topped with a few strands each of red Krystal Flash and gold Flashabou*
COLLAR: *Very webby, red saddle hackle, the butt of the saddle with the marabou-like fluff is the preferred portion of the hackle*
HEAD: *Flame orange*

This is one of the most recent of George Cook's marabou patterns. George says this is a proven B.C. and Washington winter bright fly.

WASHOUGAL OLIVE

HOOK: *Standard or low water salmon hook*
TAG: *Fine oval gold tinsel*
TAIL: *Golden-olive calftail*
BODY: *Flat gold tinsel*
RIB: *Fine oval gold tinsel*
THROAT: *Golden-olive calftail*
WING: *White calftail*

In 1968, Bill McMillan developed this pattern for the Washougal River near his home in Washington state. Tied first on the Mustad 7970, this fly was fished in the heavy early spring flows and is equally effective tied on low water hooks and fished in limited summer flows.

WINTER FLY

HOOK: *Standard salmon or steelhead hook, sizes 2-3/0*
BODY: *Flat silver tinsel*
COLLAR: *Hot orange saddle hackle*
WING: *Black hair, black bear or bucktail*

The Winter Fly was designed by Ralph Wahl. I include this fairly simple pattern because it is an attractive fly but also because it is a pattern easily converted to a dry line by substituting four black hackles for the wing and finishing it as you would the Winter's Hope.

WINTER'S HOPE

HOOK: *Large single salmon, Mustad 36890 or preferably Partridge M, sizes 1/0-6/0*
BODY: *Wide, flat silver tinsel or Mylar*
COLLAR: *Long, webby turquoise blue followed by slightly longer, webby purple hackle*
WING: *Two dark yellow hackle tips enveloped by two reddish-orange hackle tips*
TOPPING: *A few strands of golden-olive calftail*
HEAD: *Burgundy*

Bill McMillan developed this fly for use with floating lines in winter. It is designed to be fished on a deep, controlled swing. The large salmon hooks provide the only weight and will sink quite fast. This fly's shades represent a large section of the color spectrum and under low light conditions of winter show quite well. Tied on small hooks, sizes 4-8, this fly works well early morning in the summer and on sea-run cutthroats also.

WOODDUCK AND ORANGE

HOOK: *Standard salmon hook*
TAG: *Fine oval silver tinsel*
TAIL: *Dyed hot orange golden pheasant crest*
BODY: *Bright orange wool*
RIB: *Medium oval gold tinsel*
COLLAR: *Bright orange saddle followed by unbarred woodduck flank feather*
WING: *Brown bear*
CHEEKS: *Jungle cock*

Joe Howell constructs his hairwing wet flies by tying the wing in first and folding it back after everything else is done. This makes a rugged fly that holds up to many fish. His Woodduck and Orange just is one of his well-built wet flies.

ZONKER, CUTTHROAT

HOOK: *Daiichi 2441 or TMC 7999*
THREAD: *6/0 olive*
BODY: *Pearl Green Lite Brite Mylar dubbed and picked out*
RIB: *Flat silver tinsel*
COLLAR: *Short red saddle*
WING: *1/8" olive Zonker rabbit strip tied down at the rear, Zonker style*
EYES: *Nickel plated Dazl-Eyes, machined brass eyes*
HEAD: *Dubbed Lite Brite Mylar around eyes, same color as body*

The characteristic tied down rabbit strip "wing" of a Zonker is easily recognized by many fishermen. Used by bass and trout fishermen, this style of fly has proven to be very effective. Fished deep they offer the angler and the fish a good bait fish profile and with the rabbit strip wing these give a tremendous amount of subtle movement. The Cutthroat Zonker is designed by Ken Ferguson, a partner of Spirit River Inc. in Roseburg, Oregon.

Wet Flies Plate 1

Agent Orange (May)

Alexandra (Storms)

American Steelheader (Burns)

Autumn Mist (Storms)

Autumn Run (Storms)

Blackbird (Hunt)

Bluebird (Hunt)

Firebird (Hunt)

Black Demon (Helvie)

Black Gnat (Rossano)

Wet Flies Plate 2

Black Gordon (Helvie)

Black Prince (Helvie)

Black Tie (Rahr)

Blue Moon (Cook)

Boss (Helvie)

Burlap (Helvie)

Coon Mudler (Howell)

Cummings (Helvie)

Cummings Special (Burden)

Darbee Spate Fly (Rossano)

Wet Flies Plate 3

Deschutes Passion (Storms)

Deschutes Special (Howell)

Fighting Centuar (Kirchner)

Floodtide (Hunt)

Floodtide, Purple (Helvie)

Gold Ribbed Hare's Ear (Rossano)

Gold Sandy (Hunt)

Golden Demon (Helvie)

Golden Girl (Helvie)

Wet Flies Plate 4

Green Butt, Low Water (Burden)

Indian Girl (Howell)

Kandy Kane (Cook)

Lady Caroline (Kirchner)

Lunar Mist (Storms)

Lunar Run (Storms)

March Brown (Helvie)

Taluca Rabbit Muddler (Burden)

McLeod's Ugly (Helvie)

Wet Flies Plate 5

Mickey Finn (Walize)

Migrant Orange (Helvie)

Muddler Minnow (Walize)

Ondine (Kirchner)

Paint Brush (Helvie)

Payoff (Cook)

Polar Butt Black Bear, Green (Rossano)

Polar Shrimp (Helvie)

Purple Flash (Howell)

Wet Flies Plate 6

Purple Peril (Helvie)

Purple Peril, Low Water (Burden)

Purple Rat, Winter Dress (Rossano)

Rainbow Hairwing, Purple (Simpson)

Rainbow Hairwing, Blue (Simpson)

Rainbow Hairwing, Green (Simpson)

Rainbow Hairwing, Red (Simpson)

Rainbow Featherwing, Orange (Simpson)

Red Abbey, Winter Dress (Rossanno)

Wet Flies Plate 7

Red Ant (Helvie)

Red Ant Featherwing, Low Water (Burden)

Rick's Revenge (Shewey)

Royal Coachman (Helvie)

Royal Coachman (Rossano)

Royal Coachman (Kirchner)

Rusty Rat (Helvie)

S.S.S. (Gilbert)

Sacramento River Coachman (Burns)

Salmon River Purple Skunk (Burns)

Wet Flies Plate 8

Shedlock Spider, Black (Rossano)

Shedlock Spider, Brown (Rossano)

Shedlock Spider, DNA (Rossano)

Silver Ant (Helvie)

Silver Demon (Helvie)

Silver Hilton (Helvie)

Skunk (Helvie)

Skunk, Coastal (Jackson)

Skunk, Inland (Jackson)

Skunk (Kirchner)

Wet Flies Plate 9

Spade (Helvie)

Spade, Plain (Jackson)

Spade, Fancy (Jackson)

Spade, Claret Guinea (Jackson)

Spade, Yellow Guinea (Jackson)

Spade, Purple (Jackson)

Spade, Whaka Blonde (Jackson)

Spade, Jacob's Coat (Jackson)

Spruce (Helvie)

Wet Flies Plate 10

Steelhead Bear, Dark Black Bear (Rossano)   **Steelhead Bear, Dark Grizzly (Rossano)**

Black's Old Grizzly (Black)   **Black's Bunny Skunk (Black)**

Floozie (Black)

Bumble Bee Bunny (Black)

Black's Soft Candy Cain (Black)

Megan Black's Delight (Black)

Black's Swimming Sun Streak (Black)

Black's Soft Swimming Sunrise (Black)

Wet Flies Plate 11

Gold and Red Strip Wing (Hunt)

Orange and Black Strip Wing (Hunt)

Orange and Claret Strip Wing (Hunt)

Silver and Blue Strip Wing (Hunt)

Skunk Strip Wing (Hunt)

Yellow and Violet Strip Wing (Hunt)

Steelhead Woolhead (Kinney)

Steelie Bugger (Helvie)

Summer Twilight (Helvie)

Wet Flies Plate 12

The Thief is Greater than His Loot (Kirchner)

Umpqua Special (Helvie)

Undertaker (Helvie)

Volcano (Cook)

Washougal Olive (Helvie)

Winter Fly (Helvie)

Winter's Hope (Helvie)

Woodduck and Orange (Howell)

Cutthroat Zonker (Ferguson)

5
Spey Flies

JUST WHAT IS A SPEY FLY? ASK A LOT OF EXPERIENCED tiers and you will get a lot of different answers. With today's steelhead Speys it seems the only common denominator is the characteristic long, flowing hackle. Unlike the Spey flies of the mid 1800s, today's Spey fly doesn't follow many rules.

The Spey fly, as we know it, has taken many turns in its development from the simple early Spey flies designed by Scottish anglers of the 1800s for the River Spey. A. E. Knox was one, if not the first, angler of that era who tied flies resembling our Spey flies. George Kelson and other tiers of the time began expanding on the Spey style. Kelson helped to bring complexity to the Spey fly with the introduction of the Black Dog, a lavish Spey fly with jungle cock and married wings, quite uncharacteristic of most Spey flies.

It is often thought that the Spey flies A. E. Knox developed were designed to give a good impression of shrimp, a common food source of the Atlantic salmon. Many of Knox's Spey flies look very much like shrimp with the long hackle, resembling legs, and the wings of bronze mallard giving the smooth curvature of a shrimp. Most of Knox's Spey flies were quite somber in color by today's standards. Nonetheless, early Spey flies such as the Lady Caroline are still very effective.

Another facet of today's steelhead Spey that should be discussed is the Dee Strip Wing fly. The Dee Strip Wing is another native of Scotland and the River Dee in Aberdeenshire. The Dee fly is an even older style than the Spey, dating back to the 1700s. There are many distinctive differences between the Dee and the Spey yet on today's steelhead Spey flies many of these differences overlap.

Dee Strip Wing flies were generally more colorful and intricate than the Spey fly but there were always exceptions to this rule. The Black Dog was one Spey fly that was an exception and even today is very popular with both the Atlantic salmon fly tier and the steelhead angler.

Unlike the more traditional Spey flies of the past 150 years, Dee flies almost always had bodies of several sections of seal or floss like today's steelhead Spey. Dee and Spey flies of the past were usually tied on extra long shank hooks, 3XL or 4XL, and sometimes longer. Today's steelhead Spey flies are often tied on a slightly longer hook but not quite that long.

The hackles on both the Spey and the Dee were long and flowing, often heron feather, either black or gray. Today's steelhead Spey fly also has the characteristic long body hackle, but because of current laws substitutions are made for the heron. Blue eared pheasant is one of the most widely used replacement feathers. The texture is slightly softer than that of heron, the stem is noticeably finer and much easier to work with.

Fullness of the hackle is up to the individual tier. The original Spey flies were tied sparsely in Spey hackle. One way to achieve this is to strip one side of the hackle before winding. I personally prefer a sparser fly and always strip the Spey hackle first. Some tiers prefer a fuller fly and double the feather; some want it fuller yet and use two or three Spey feathers to get the effect they want.

Some time ago I began playing around with different substitutes for heron feathers. Several feathers proved to be quite useful as a Spey hackle. Flank feathers from many ducks and geese work well if processed properly. By burning the flue from the feathers with a chlorine bleach solution they lose their web and become heron-like. Mix one part bleach to two parts water and swish the feather around for about a minute and a half to remove the flue. Experiment with a few feathers and keep fresh water on hand to rinse the feather so the burning does not continue after you are through. Colors are also added to Spey hackle; orange, purple and red are just a few used on Spey flies today. Flank feathers can be dyed after they are burned and white feathers dye well to solid light colors. The biggest drawback to using flank feathers is their large diameter and stiffness of stem.

Marabou makes functional and attractive Spey hackles, as long as the right feathers are chosen. Look for feathers with the finest stem possible and the least amount of flue. Again, I prefer to strip one side of the feather before tying it in. I always tie them in by the tip. Be careful: they can be fragile. Counter wrapping the marabou with fine wire or burying the stem under the rib greatly improves the durability of the fly, regardless of the feather chosen for the Spey hackle. Because of all the colors available in marabou, the Spey fly tier can be very creative converting standard wet fly patterns to marabou Spey flies.

When the wings on both the Spey and Dee fly are studied, vast differences are found. Spey fly wings, for the most part, were made of a soft fibered duck shoulder, bronze mallard being the most prevalent. They were often specified to be "dark mallard with light colored roots," the roots being the butt end of the wing next to the head. The wings form a smooth tent over the back of the fly enveloping the upper side of the fly.

Dee flies, on the other hand, had wings made of firmer feathers. Turkey tails of varying colors were used almost exclusively. The method for setting these wings was drastically different. Dee wings were set flat over the body, extending just past the end of the hook and forming a "V" with the two wings. The Dee style wing is confusing to many tiers, as the exact method of attaching the wings varies greatly. Today, this style of wing can range from the traditional flat method to a modified Dee wing that is somewhat tented, almost a cross between a Dee and Spey wing. The true, flat Dee is the style of wing I am referring to when a "Dee style" wing is mentioned.

The steelhead Spey uses several styles and materials in constructing the wing. Goose shoulder strips in single and multiple colors are very common in modern Spey flies. Whole feather-wings of hackle tips, pheasant tippets and duck flank feathers are used on today's Spey fly, something that very few Spey or Dee flies of previous centuries had. These wings are also set in varying styles, from true Dee style to true Spey style, with many alternate methods in between.

Luckily, we are not bound by unwritten rules guiding our Spey fly designs. The steelhead Spey is a well-balanced blend of both the traditional Spey and Dee fly with a whole lot of Yankee ingenuity thrown in to provide a home-grown breed of "Spey fly," unique in many ways. To many purists the hairwing Spey is a contradiction in terms. How could you have a classic Spey fly with a hairwing? Several innovative tiers have developed some very attractive hairwing Spey flies. These flies are a great compromise between the functional beauty of the Spey fly and the ruggedness of a hairwing.

Cheeks, toppings and horns, along with other adornments, are commonplace on the steelhead Spey. All of these ornaments, along with a nearly endless palette of colors, are what have helped create a class of fly which is second to none in function and beauty. The steelhead Spey will be a classic for years to come.

> The first Spey fly demonstrated will be a Gray Heron. A light wire, longer shank hook works well for this pattern. A Partridge Bartleet is shown.

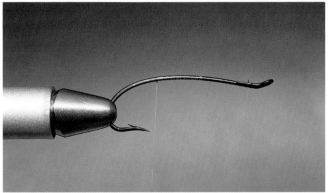

Step 1: Attach your thread and wind it back to above the point of the hook. I use unwaxed thread and start with a light color, white or yellow. Unwaxed thread lies flat and gives a smooth underbody.

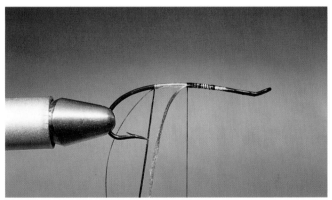

Step 2: Tie in a piece of fine oval silver tinsel and a piece of narrow flat silver tinsel. Move the thread forward about one-third of the way up the shank and tie in a single strand of yellow floss. Switch threads to a black unwaxed thread.

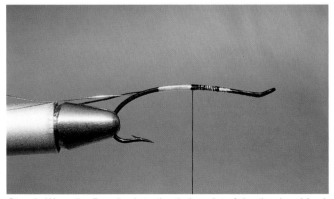

Step 3: Wrap the floss back to the tie-in point of the tinsel and back again, making sure that the floss lies flat, achieving a thin body section.

Step 4: Tie in a Spey hackle, by the tip, on the underside of the shank. Blue eared pheasant is used for this demonstration. Flatten the thread by letting it untwist, and separate the thread evenly with a bodkin. This will be your dubbing loop.

Step 5: Wax this separated thread, about three to four inches.

Step 6: Place a small amount of seal or goat in the formed loop (the dubbing should be thin) and spin the bobbin to tighten the loop.

Step 7: Wind this forward to about 3/16 of an inch from the eye. The dubbing should stop on the thread at the same point. This takes a little practice.

Step 8: Wind the tinsels forward five turns, having the oval tinsel trail the flat. End with the tinsels being tied off on the underside of the hook—this helps keep the wing from going on crooked.

Step 9: Strip the left side of the Spey feather, about half to two-thirds from the tip (or tie-in point) back.

Step 10: Wind the hackle behind the ribs to the tie-off point of the tinsel. Fold the remaining hackle over and take a turn or two at the shoulder depending on how full you want the hackle, covering up the tinsel tie-off, and tie off.

Step 11: Trim the hackle off closely and tie in a soft guinea hen feather by the tip. Fold it in half and take a turn or two of it and tie off, trimming closely. I find a razor blade or scalpel works best for trimming the stem.

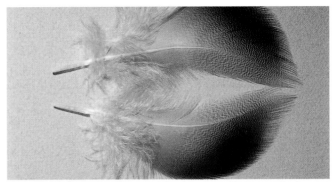

Step 12: Find a pair of bronze mallard feathers that are not wispy on the ends. Good feathers are tight and cling to themselves. Original Spey patterns called for "mallard with light roots and dark tips," the greater the contrast the better. Lay these feathers out in front of you, curving inward with the bronze color on the outside. The left feather is for the near wing and vice versa, provided you are tying right-handed.

Step 13: Strip off the useless side of the feathers and the lower fluff. Take the lower quarter inch of each feather and pull the fibers downward, but not off the stem! Stroke the sections downward and smooth them out, giving them a gentle curve as you go.

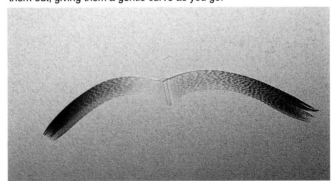

Step 14: Snip off that section of feather, stem and all. The stem helps hold the feather together.

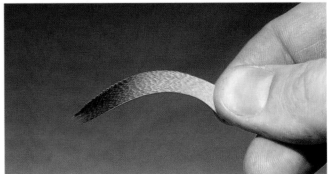

Step 15: Be sure the feathers you choose are well matched, hold the stems together with your right thumb and index finger. Stroke the feathers together and downward. This is what your wing will look like on the fly.

Step 16: Saddle the tented wing sections over the hook, the Spey fly mallard wing should set low and tent the upper half of the fly. Holding the wings with your left hand, take a couple of soft loops over the wing butts. Slowly tighten the soft loops while pinching the wing butts with your finger and thumb. Using unwaxed thread will help prevent the thread from grabbing and rolling the wings over, a problem with bronze mallard wings. Inspect the wings. If they look good, snug them down, put a couple of drops of thin cement on the butts and let them dry.

Step 17: After the cement has dried a couple of minutes, trim the butts of the wing with a razor. Wind a small head and whip finish and cement. The finished Gray Heron.

Another common style of Spey wing is the hackle tip wing, as on the Orange Heron. We will pick up on the wing of this fly, the rest of the methods are about the same.

Step 1: Select four small neck or saddle hackles and remove the fluff. You should have two pairs, curving slightly the opposite direction.

Step 2: The wing should be about the length of the body or a little longer and curve downward slightly.

Step 3: The wing feathers should have about an inch and a half of fine, bare stem. Take a small pair of pliers and flatten the stems at the tie-in point.

Step 4: Insert the stems of the feathers into the eye of the hook, making sure the feathers stay even and in order. Take two or three tight turns of thread and add a drop of thin cement.

Step 5: Pull the stems down and back through the groove between the looped eye. Pull snug but don't pull the wing loose. Lay the stems under the fly and take a couple of turns of thread to bind them down.

STEELHEAD FLY TYING GUIDE

Step 6: Trim the stems off closely, finish the head small and the Orange Heron is complete. This method of tying in hackle wings insures the wing is in solidly and allows for a small head. I use this method when tying any hackle wings such as on a Spruce or Silver Hilton. You must use a quality hook with a well tapered eye, however.

The final style of Spey wing I show is the Dee style wing. Although the Dee is a style all in itself, steelheaders have integrated it into Spey flies. Many 19th century authors failed to give detailed instructions on Dee wings. The style of Dee wing I show is correct from what I have been able to gather from early books and writings. Other tiers may have different ideas on what a Dee wing is.

Dee wings should lay flat over the body and extend to the bend of the hook. They are set in a "V" fashion, splaying away from each other slightly, allowing for greater movement. Straight fibered feathers, such as turkey tails, work best but good quality white turkey is difficult to obtain and goose shoulder is often used instead. I show this style of wing on the Akroyd.

Step 1: Start with a pair of goose shoulders or turkey tails (I chose turkey). When using turkey tails, you can often find single feathers that are even on both sides and only one feather is required. This style of wing is the opposite of most regarding which feather, or side of the feather, is for which wing. Setting the feather out in front as before, the left side is for the far wing and vice versa. With the fly ready for the wing, cut a quarter-inch section out of the outside section of each feather or both sides of a single, even turkey tail.

Step 2: I find it easier to attach the far wing first and the near wing second. If you have a rotary vise, turn the head slightly towards you; this will help attach the wing easier. Lay the strip from the left quill or side on top of the fly, flat, and take a single turn of thread over the wing butt, tighten it down slowly, positioning it as you go. Take a couple more turns when you get the wing in position.

Step 3: Turn the head of the vise back to the upright position. Take the other strip and attach it in the same manner as the first, positioning it as you go. Take a couple of tight turns after the wing is in position. Add a drop of cement to the butts and let dry.

Step 4: Trim the butts of the wings closely with a razor.

Step 5: Tie in a pair of jungle cock eyes on each side, pointing down and back slightly (drooping). Flattening the stems of the eyes with a pair of pliers will help keep them from rolling.

Step 6: Trim off the stems, finish the head and the Akroyd is done.

Plate 1 Page 72

APPLE MAGGOT SPEY

HOOK: Alec Jackson Spey Hook, nickel, sizes 3-7
TAG: Copper wire, fine
BODY: Rear two thirds yellow floss; front third yellow African goat fur
RIB: Copper wire, fine
HACKLE: Brown Chinese pheasant rump
THROAT: Yellow guinea hen
WING: Four burnt orange hackle tips
HEAD: White or yellow

Scott O'Donnell developed this pattern for bright days and gin clear water, he named it for the apple orchard he fished through when he first used this fly.

AUTUMN SKIES NO. 2

HOOK: Bartleet style Spey hook or low water style, sizes 3/0-2
TAG: Flat silver tinsel, optional
BODY: In four equal sections, starting with bright orange silk floss followed by fluorescent floss and equal sections of flame red seal and purple seal
RIB: Wide flat gold tinsel with a counter wrap of fine oval gold tinsel to help protect the hackle
HACKLE: Three Spey hackles: flame red and bright orange starting at the red seal and purple starting with the purple seal; all three hackles over the purple seal
COLLAR: One turn of the purple Spey hackle
WINGS: Deep purple goose shoulder or swan with a narrow strip (two strands) of bright red goose or swan married in the center; tie these in low and tented over the body—the tips of the wings should meet above the tail
HEAD: Bright red

This is one of John Shewey's many creations. If a sparser fly is desired, John says to strip one side of the Spey hackles.

BEDSPRINGS SPEY

HOOK: Bartleet style Spey hook, Partridge or Alec Jackson, sizes 1/0-4
TAG: One-third flat gold tinsel and two-thirds fluorescent orange floss
TAIL: Hot orange golden pheasant crest
BODY: Rear half orange seal or goat fur; front half deep brown seal or goat
RIB: Flat gold tinsel followed by oval gold tinsel; counter wrap with fine gold wire to reinforce the hackle
HACKLE: Black heron substitute over brown seal's fur along ribs
COLLAR: Black Spey hackle followed by gadwall or hooded merganser flank
WING: Bronze mallard tented low over the body

John Shewey devised this dark Spey fly. John is a very talented tier and writer from Aumsville, Oregon.

BELVEDERE

HOOK: Alec Jackson Spey Hook, sizes 1 1/2-5 or Bartleet
TAG: Flat red Mylar tinsel approximately one-third body length
TAIL: Golden pheasant crest dyed red
BODY: Black seal or goat fur
RIB: Red Mylar tinsel over body and oval silver tinsel over body and tag
HACKLE: Black Chinese pheasant dyed black over seal's fur behind ribs
THROAT: Claret guinea hen
WING: Black goose strips set low and tented
CHEEKS: Small jungle cock
HEAD: Wine

This good, dark fly was sent to me by Dec Hogan from Mt. Vernon, Washington.

BLACK JACK

HOOK: Alec Jackson Spey Hook
TAG: Flat gold tinsel
BODY: Black floss
RIB: Fine oval gold tinsel
HACKLE: Gray heron substitute, from the second turn of tinsel
COLLAR: Guinea hen
WING: Argus pheasant tail strips
CHEEKS: Jungle cock, drooping
HEAD: Black

Joe Howell and his wife Bonnie run the Blue Heron Fly Shop on the North Umpqua River near Idleyld Park, Oregon. For several years Joe and I have competed in the retail business. During that time Joe has always been helpful and never shown any animosity towards me or my business. Joe is a class act. I consider him a friend and can talk with him about work or personal things. Very seldom do you find a competitor about whom you can find nothing bad to say, except that he is too good a fisherman.

Joe's Spey flies are meticulously tied. They are both pleasing to the eye and well-constructed. Any of Joe's Spey flies could be framed or fished with confidence that they will hold together. Joe ties his flies to be fished with, yet he is able to incorporate grace and beauty into each fly.

BRAD'S BRAT SPEY

HOOK: Alec Jackson Spey Hook, sizes 1 1/2-5
TAG: Medium flat gold tinsel
TAIL: Dyed orange golden pheasant crest
BODY: Rear half orange floss; front half red seal or substitute
RIB: Fine oval gold tinsel
HACKLE: Gray Spey hackle over red seal only
COLLAR: Hooded merganser or widgeon
WING: Two pairs of white hackle tips
CHEEKS: Jungle cock
TOPPING: Dyed orange golden pheasant crest

Enos Bradner's fly Brad's Brat has bred many variations but this Spey fly by Brad Burden is the nicest looking one I have seen. A very graceful and fishable pattern.

BROWN HERON

HOOK: Low water salmon or Spey hook
BODY: Rear two-thirds hot orange floss; hot orange seal's fur for the remainder
RIB: Flat and oval silver tinsel
HACKLE: Gray heron or substitute, with one side stripped, wrapped along ribs
THROAT: Teal flank, 1 1/2 turns
WINGS: Bronze mallard or widgeon flank strips set low and tented
HEAD: Red thread

This is one of Syd Glasso's flies in the Heron series. Syd and Dick Wentworth helped to develop the Spey fly for the Northwest steelhead angler.

BLACK DEMON SPEY

HOOK: Bartleet style salmon hook
BODY: Rear half flat silver tinsel; front half black seal or goat
RIB: Flat and fine oval silver tinsel
HACKLE: Black heron substitute over seal's fur
COLLAR: Red guinea hen, 1 1/2 turns
WINGS: Four red hackle tips or goose strips set low

This is one of the author's patterns. It's a good summer or winter fly depending on the size, up to 3/0 or even larger.

CALEB'S SCREAMER

HOOK: Daiichi 6XL streamer hook; remove eye and tie blind-eyed with 20-pound Dacron or silk gut for eye
TAG: Fine oval silver tinsel
TAIL: Golden pheasant crest dyed red
BUTT: Black ostrich herl
BODY: Rear half flat silver tinsel; front half black seal or substitute; veil above and below at joint with red parrot or macaw body feathers
RIB: Rear half closely ribbed, seven turns, with fine oval silver tinsel; rib front half with flat red Mylar followed by oval silver tinsel
HACKLE: Long, black heron substitute over seal's fur
COLLAR: Gadwall flank and then golden pheasant flank dyed red
WING: Amherst pheasant center tail strips set flat, Dee style
CHEEKS: Jungle cock set horizontally
HORNS: Two red macaw tail fibers set low and drooping
HEAD: Small black

This is the fanciest of my fishing Spey/Dee flies. While it may seem like overkill to many, it is a good large fly for deep summer water or lower winter water. It has a good profile yet with the heavy Daiichi hook it sinks well on a floating line. I fish it with a gut or Dacron eye for the extra movement they provide. My son, Caleb, was a newborn when I first tied this fly, thus, the name.

CARRON

HOOK: Bartleet style Spey hook or low water salmon
BODY: Orange floss
RIB: Red floss with two strands of fine oval silver tinsel, one on each side of the floss
HACKLE: Black heron substitute from the end of the body, along the ribs
COLLAR: Teal flank, 1 1/2 turns
WING: Bronze mallard

This is my adaptation of an old standard 1800s Spey fly. The original pattern uses wool for the body and a slightly different application of the rib.

Plate 2 Page 73

CHAPPIE SPEY

HOOK: Alec Jackson Spey or Bartleet style or any low water hook
TAG: Flat gold tinsel
TAIL: Mallard, teal or gadwall flank fibers
BODY: Rear third hot orange floss; front two-thirds hot orange seal's fur or substitute
RIB: Flat gold tinsel with fine oval gold tinsel behind
HACKLE: Large mallard flank feather, burned to remove flue; strip one side, tie in by the tip and wrap over fur behind ribs; large gadwall flank feathers work well also
COLLAR: Long grizzly
WING: Four grizzly hackle tips set low
HEAD: Hot orange

This is a variation I developed in 1991 of the traditional pattern that "Outdoor" Franklin introduced in 1940. It is an attractive bright fly with somber hackle and wings that works well in smaller sizes, 4 and 6, for summer or as large as the mallard flank will allow for spring and winter fish.

CLARET AND BLACK DEE

HOOK: Partridge Bartlett, sizes 1/0-3/0, modified blind eye
EYE: 20-pound Dacron loop eye
THREAD: Yellow 6/0
TAG: Flat silver tinsel
TAIL: Golden pheasant crest and tippet strands
BODY: Rear half claret seal's fur; front half black seal's fur
RIB: Medium oval silver tinsel over each section
HACKLE: Claret saddle hackle over claret seal, dyed black pheasant hackle over black seal
COLLAR: Widgeon
WING: Cinnamon turkey tail strips set Dee style or Spey style
CHEEKS: Jungle cock set low, drooping
HEAD: Black 6/0 thread

Greg Scot Hunt's Claret and Black Dee is reminiscent of the Akroyd and Jock O'Dee of Atlantic salmon use. Greg uses this and other Dee style patterns on winter steelhead.

CLARET SPEY

HOOK: Alec Jackson Spey Hook with the eye straightened out, blind-eye, sizes 6-1 1/2
EYE: Silk gut or braided Dacron loop
BODY: Claret, seal or goat, thin
RIB: Medium oval and flat gold tinsel wrapped equidistant to each other with an extra-fine oval silver tinsel counter wrap
HACKLE: Claret Spey hackle
THROAT: Guinea hen
WING: Bronze mallard, set Spey style
HEAD: Claret

Karen Gobin of Marysville, Washington developed this attractive fly. Her husband, Steve tied this sample for me along very classic lines. This is a good midday spring pattern and produced a 14-pound fish on its first use.

DEEP PURPLE SPEY (Gobin)

HOOK: Alec Jackson Spey Hook, sizes 6-1/0, with the eye straightened out, blind eye
EYE: Silk gut or braided Dacron loop
BODY: Purple seal or substitute, thin
RIB: Medium oval silver and medium flat gold tinsel wrapped equidistant with an extra-fine oval silver tinsel counter wrap
HACKLE: Purple Spey hackle
THROAT: Guinea hen
WING: Bronze mallard, tented low
HEAD: Claret

Steve Gobin is one of the West coast's finest fly tiers. His Spey flies are impeccable and his full-dressed Salmon flies are true works of art. This pattern, says Steve, is used in spring and early summer when high clear water is present, smaller sizes later.

DEEP PURPLE SPEY (Johnson)

HOOK: Spey or low water salmon, originally tied on Wilson dry fly salmon hook
BODY: Deep purple mohair wool
RIB: Flat silver tinsel
HACKLE: Dark brown Chinese pheasant rump, doubled, from the second turn of tinsel
COLLAR: Long, webby deep purple hackle
WING: A pair of red golden pheasant flank feathers set low

This is one of Walt Johnson's Spey patterns. The purple is effective in almost any condition, summer or winter.

DEEPENDABLE SERIES

Joe Rossano of Seattle, Washington ties his Deependable series to be fished deep, thus the name "Deep" endable. Joe is a displaced eastterner who has brought a lot of his Atlantic salmon experience with him. He uses schlappen in the body of these flies to help hold the marabou away from the body when in the water. Joe is an innovative, first class tier whose work is very meticulous.

DEEPENDABLE, BLUE (IMPROVED)

HOOK: *Bartleet, sizes up to 3/0*
THREAD: *Blue*
TAG: *Fine oval silver tinsel*
TAIL: *Yellow golden pheasant rump feather*
BODY: *Rear half black leech yarn; front half bright blue schlappen wound tight; tie in by the tip and use the whole feather, including the fluff*
RIB: *Embossed silver tinsel over the black yarn*
COLLAR: *Long, black marabou, several turns; followed by a turn or two of teal*
WING: *Brown turkey strips*
HEAD: *Blue*

This pattern is a consistent fish catcher, according to Joe. The dark color and mobility make it a great winter fly. Joe ties these flies larger on low water hooks.

DEEPENDABLE, GLED WING

HOOK: *Bartleet, up to 3/0, or low water*
THREAD: *Red*
TAG: *Fine oval silver tinsel*
TAIL: *Golden pheasant breast feather*
BODY: *Rear half yellow mohair or Angora goat; front half purple schlappen packed in tightly; tie in the feather by the tip and wind, using the entire feather, including the fluff*
RIB: *Embossed silver tinsel over the rear half of the body*
COLLAR: *Several turns of black marabou followed by one or two turns of teal*
WING: *Brown turkey strips*
HEAD: *Red*

Joe uses the old Gled Wing as the basis for this pattern. The original Gled Wing was a Dee strip wing pattern and appeared in Francis Francis' work, *A Book on Angling,* in 1867.

DEEPENDABLE, TARTAN

HOOK: *Bartleet, up to 3/0, or low water*
THREAD: *Red*
TAG: *Fine oval silver tinsel*
TAIL: *Yellow, golden pheasant rump feather*
BODY: *Rear half orange leech yarn; front half red schlappen packed tightly; tie in the feather by the tip and use the entire feather including the fluff*
RIB: *Large flat gold tinsel over the rear half of the body only*
HACKLE: *Soft natural red cock's hackle over orange yarn, along ribs*
COLLAR: *Several turns of natural brown turkey marabou followed by a turn or two of teal*
WING: *White turkey strips set Dee style*
HEAD: *Red*

This pattern was also based on an early Dee Strip wing fly of the 1800s.

DEE'S DEMON

HOOK: *Medium to heavy single salmon or Bartleet style, sizes 3/0-2*
TAIL: *Red golden pheasant crest*
TAG: *Flat gold tinsel*
BODY: *Rear half orange seal or goat; front half dark brown seal or goat*
RIB: *Flat gold tinsel, wide or medium, followed by fine, oval gold tinsel, counter wrapped with fine oval gold tinsel*
HACKLE: *One black and one orange Spey hackle through the black fur only*
COLLAR: *Same black as the body Spey hackle*
UNDERWING: *Two long jungle cock between two golden pheasant tippets*
WING: *One pair hooded merganser flank feathers veiling the underwing*
CHEEKS: *Medium jungle cock lying along the stem of the wing feathers*
TOPPING: *Golden pheasant crest*
HEAD: *Black with narrow orange band next to the wing*

John Shewey developed this pattern, one of the few Spey flies that does not have the low-setting wing characteristic of most Spey flies. Many of John's patterns are on the cutting edge of today's flies.

DESERT STORM

HOOK: *Alec Jackson Spey Hook*
TAG: *Flat silver tinsel*
TAIL: *Dyed red golden pheasant crest*
BUTT: *Black ostrich herl*
BODY: *Danville's soldier blue floss*
RIB: *Fine oval silver tinsel*
HACKLE: *Black Spey hackle, from the second turn of tinsel*
COLLAR: *Dyed blue guinea hen*
WING: *Married strips of goose shoulder; starting at the top: red, white and blue; set low*
CHEEKS: *Jungle cock, drooping*
HEAD: *Black*

Joe Howell created this patriotic pattern in honor of the Gulf War. It will catch fish, too!

Plate 3 Page 74

DICOS SPEY

HOOK: *Alec Jackson Spey Hook, gold or black, sizes 3 or 5*
BODY: *Rear half flat gold tinsel; front half orange seal fur*
RIB: *Fine oval gold tinsel*
HACKLE: *Extra large golden pheasant flank feather over seal*
COLLAR: *Yellow golden pheasant rump feather, 1 1/2 turns, followed by one turn of woodduck flank feather*
WING: *Matching strips of mottled oak turkey*
HEAD: *Red*

This is a pattern I designed after the colors of the October caddis, *Dicosmoecus,* which is how I came up with the name. Fished greased line, this pattern can really move fish when the bugs are out.

DOUBLE EAGLE SPEY

HOOK: *Bartleet or low water, sizes 3/0-2*
THREAD: *Bright orange*
TAG: *Flat gold tinsel, optional*
BODY: *Rear half orange silk floss; front half orange seal*
RIB: *Wide, flat gold tinsel trailed by fine oval gold tinsel*
HACKLE: *Eagle imitation, webby marabou, one each of natural brown-gray and orange or speckled orange, over seal's fur only, behind ribs; stripping one side of each hackle will prevent the fly from being overly full*
COLLAR: *Gadwall flank*
WING: *Narrow strips of dyed orange mallard shoulder, set low*
CHEEKS: *Jungle cock, optional*
HEAD: *Bright orange*

During the peak of the Victorian age of Atlantic salmon fishing in the United Kingdom, patterns using eagle hackles were popular. The Gray Eagle, Yellow Eagle and Quilled Eagle were a few standards of the time. John Shewey's Double Eagle is a bright pattern along the lines of this classic style.

FIRE ANT SPEY

HOOK: *Alec Jackson Spey Hook, sizes 1 1/2-5*
TAG: *Medium flat silver tinsel*
TAIL: *Dyed red golden pheasant crest*
BODY: *Rear third red floss; front two-thirds black seal or goat*
RIB: *Fine oval silver tinsel*
HACKLE: *Long, black Spey hackle over seal only*
COLLAR: *Dyed red teal flank feather*
WING: *Natural red, golden pheasant body feathers*
CHEEKS: *Jungle cock*
TOPPING: *Dyed red golden pheasant crest*
HEAD: *Black*

FIRE PLUM SPEY

HOOK: *Alec Jackson Spey Hook, sizes 1 1/2-5*
TAG: *Medium flat silver tinsel*
TAIL: *Dyed purple golden pheasant crest*
BODY: *Rear third red floss; front two-thirds purple seal or goat*
RIB: *Fine oval silver tinsel*
HACKLE: *Long, black Spey hackle over seal's fur only*
COLLAR: *Dyed red teal flank feather*
WING: *Dyed purple golden pheasant body feathers*
CHEEKS: *Jungle cock*
TOPPING: *Dyed purple golden pheasant crest*
HEAD: *Black*

The Fire Ant and the Fire Plum Spey are the work of Brad Burden, a skilled tier from Portland, Oregon.

FLOODTIDE SPEY

HOOK: *Bartleet style Spey hook or Partridge N low water*
TAG: *Fine oval silver tinsel and red floss*
TAIL: *Golden pheasant crest*
BUTT: *Black ostrich herl*
BODY: *One fourth each of yellow floss, yellow, orange and red seal's fur at the shoulder*
RIB: *Fine oval silver and fine flat silver tinsel*
HACKLE: *Golden yellow marabou plume, one side stripped, palmered behind ribs over seal's fur only*
COLLAR: *Red guinea hen, 1 1/2 turns*
WING: *Married strips of yellow and red goose shoulder and peacock wing set horizon tally and flat, Dee style*
CHEEKS: *Jungle cock, drooping*

The Floodtide was originally an 1800s full-dressed Atlantic salmon fly designed for high water. Back when anything was legal, bustard and eagle feathers were commonplace on many salmon flies. For economic and legal reasons, I use peacock and marabou on this pattern.

FLOODTIDE SPEY, PURPLE

HOOK: *Bartleet style Spey hook or Partridge N low water*
TAG: *Fine oval silver tinsel and red floss*
TAIL: *Golden pheasant crest*
BUTT: *Black ostrich herl*
BODY: *Equal sections each pale fluorescent orange floss and orange, red and purple seal's fur*
RIB: *Fine oval silver and fine flat silver tinsel*
HACKLE: *Purple marabou, fine stemmed, one side stripped, over seal's fur only, behind ribs*
COLLAR: *Red guinea hen, 1 1/2 turns*
WING: *Married strips of purple and orange goose shoulder and peacock wing*
CHEEKS: *Jungle cock, drooping*

The purple version of this pattern is a good low light pattern. With marabou it has a lot of movement.

GOLD HERON

HOOK: *Low water or Bartleet style Spey hook*
BODY: *Rear two-thirds flat gold tinsel; front third orange seal or substitute*
RIB: *Fine oval gold tinsel*
HACKLE: *Brown or heron substitute over seal's fur behind ribs*
COLLAR: *Widgeon flank, sparse, 1 1/2 turns*
WINGS: *Widgeon flank tented over body set low, traditional Spey style*
HEAD: *Orange thread, small*

The late Syd Glasso developed this fly in his Heron series for winter steelhead on the Olympic Peninsula. His exquisite Spey flies helped to set the standard in fly tying. He normally tied his flies on size 1 or 2 English style low water hooks for his winter and early spring fishing.

GOLDEN DEMON SPEY

HOOK: *Alec Jackson Spey Hook, sizes 1 1/2-5*
TAG: *Medium flat gold tinsel*
TAIL: *Golden pheasant crest*
BODY: *Medium flat gold tinsel*
RIB: *Fine oval gold tinsel*
HACKLE: *Dyed orange Spey hackle*
COLLAR: *Dyed orange guinea*
WING: *Bronze mallard strips over an underwing of two badger hackle tips dyed brown*
CHEEKS: *Jungle cock*
TOPPING: *Two golden pheasant crests*

This flashy version of the Golden Demon, made famous by Zane Grey and Jim Pray, is a product of Brad Burden's creative mind. Being compact and with its tinsel construction and featherwings, it will sink and swim very well.

GRAY HERON

HOOK: *Bartleet style Spey Hook*
BODY: *Rear third lemon floss; front two-thirds black seal*
RIB: *Medium flat silver tinsel followed by fine oval silver tinsel*
HACKLE: *Gray heron substitute from the second turn of tinsel*
COLLAR: *Guinea hen, 1 1/2 turns*
WING: *Bronze mallard strips set low*

This ancient pattern was first used on Atlantic salmon on the River Spey around 1850. The original version of A. E. Knox's pattern used wool for the body but I prefer the floss and seal combination. The pattern shown has a twisted gut eye on a Partridge blind-eyed Bartleet hook.

HOT PEACOCK SPEY

HOOK: *Alec Jackson Spey Hook, sizes 1 1/2-5*
TAG: *Fine oval silver tinsel*
BODY: *Rear third fluorescent red floss; front two-thirds peacock herl; twist herl with thread to form a chenille*
RIB: *Fine oval silver tinsel*
HACKLE: *Gray Spey hackle, over peacock only*
COLLAR: *Teal flank feather; green wing teal is preferred because of its finer markings*
WING: *Bronze mallard strips set low over body*
HEAD: *Black*

The Hot Peacock Spey is a creation of Brad Burden, who utilizes materials very well in his patterns. Peacock herl bodies are seldom seen on Spey flies but work well when trying to achieve flash and movement with the natural materials often associated with Spey flies.

JUNGLE COCK ROCK

HOOK: *Alec Jackson Spey Hook, size 3*
BODY: *None*
UNDERWING: *Small bunch of dyed orange squirrel slightly beyond the bend and cocked up slightly, followed by a few strands, ends uneven, well beyond the hook bend; keep it sparse*
HACKLE: *Dyed orange pheasant rump feather tied by the tip, followed by dyed black pheasant rump tied in the same manner*
WING: *Brown-tipped flank feather from jungle cock, one from each side, tied on each side of hook extending just beyond the bend*
CHEEKS: *Jungle cock*
COLLAR: *Black and white feather from the base of the jungle cock neck, tied in by the tip and folded, two turns*
HEAD: *Wine thread*

Dec Hogan of Mt. Vernon, Washington says of his Jungle Cock Rock "The Jungle Cock Rock has proven to be an excellent fall pattern in relatively clear water, good as a search pattern or cast to spotted fish. The take is always violent and deliberate. An outstanding follow up fly, it seems to take fish when other patterns won't. Although it has only been tested in the fall, I feel that in seasons to come it will prove to be a good producer throughout the year."

Plate 4 Page 75

LADY CAROLINE

HOOK: *Traditional low water salmon or Bartleet style Spey hook*
TAIL: *Golden pheasant breast feather fibers*
BODY: *Blended seal's fur, one part olive green, two parts light brown*
RIBS: *Flat gold tinsel followed by fine oval silver tinsel; fine gold wire counter wraps the body hackle (often omitted)*
HACKLE: *Gray heron substitute behind ribs from tail*
THROAT: *Golden pheasant breast feather*
WING: *Bronze mallard strips set low*
HEAD: *Black*

The originator of the Lady Caroline is unknown. This drab yet beautiful Spey fly dates back well into the 1800s. This is one of the few truly old Atlantic salmon patterns that has survived the test of time and is still popular with steelhead anglers. My first introduction to this pattern for steelhead was by Ray Zalunardo, biologist for the Forest Service. Ray praised the Lady Caroline for quite some time before I took much notice of the fly. For summer and fall fish in clear water this nonglaring pattern is hard to beat.

Many early dressings call for fine oval gold tinsel instead of wire and it is often not counter wrapped with the three ribs wound the same direction, equal distances apart. There is also a nonSpey dressing for this fly in the standard fly section for those who want a simpler tie of this useful fly.

LEGAL EAGLE

HOOK: *Partridge Bartleet or Alec Jackson Spey Hook*
BODY: *Rear third flat silver tinsel; front two-thirds equal sections of orange, red and purple seal or substitute*
RIB: *Fine oval silver tinsel; counter rib with fine silver wire*
HACKLE: *Two fluffy, fine stemmed marabou quills, one each purple and red/orange; strip one side and tie them in by the tip, palmered along the ribs over the seal's fur only*
COLLAR: *Peacock pheasant saddle feather or guinea hen*
WING: *Bronze mallard*
HEAD: *Red*

Atlantic salmon fly tiers know the Eagles very well. During the Victorian age, they had eagle hackles for the body feathers and were quite popular in the mid to late 1800s. The use of eagle feathers is now illegal so we use turkey marabou. I developed this pattern for some of the deep, slow stretches of the North Umpqua River.

McJONES

HOOK: *Alec Jackson Spey Hook*
BODY: *Rear third burgundy floss; balance black seal's fur*
RIB: *Small silver tinsel*
HACKLE: *Gray heron substitute tied in by the tip and wound behind ribs*
THROAT: *Dyed burgundy guinea hen*
WING: *Four matching golden pheasant breast feathers dyed purple, set low; when dyed purple these feathers are a blackish/burgundy*
CHEEKS: *Small jungle cock eyes*
HEAD: *Wine thread*

This fly got its name after some British clients decided that their guiding partner Dec Hogan needed a "proper title" and dubbed him "McJones." Again, dark flies are a major part of any guide's arsenal. This fly is a good one.

MARABOU SPEY FLIES

ADMIRAL MARABOU

HOOK: *Bartleet style Spey hook or low water salmon, sizes up to 4/0 for winter use*
TAG: *Flat silver tinsel*
TAIL: *Dyed red golden pheasant crest*
BODY: *Rear third red floss; remainder red seal's fur or substitute*
RIB: *Flat silver tinsel with oval silver tinsel behind*
HACKLE: *Red marabou, fine stemmed, wound along ribs over seal; strip one side first*
COLLAR: *Gadwall flank, 1 1/2 turns*
WING: *White goose shoulder or swan strips set flat and splayed slightly, Dee style*
CHEEKS: *Jungle cock, drooping*
HEAD: *Red*

A highly visible pattern that gives the appearance of bulk though it is actually quite sparse. My simple marabou conversion gives a lot of movement to an old standard fly.

BLACK GORDON MARABOU SPEY

HOOK: *Bartleet style Spey hook or low water, in larger sizes for winter use*
TAG: *Fine oval gold tinsel*
BODY: *Rear third red floss; front two-thirds black seal's fur*
RIB: *Fine oval gold tinsel*
HACKLE: *Black marabou over seal, one side stripped*
COLLAR: *Gadwall*
WING: *Black goose shoulder or swan strips, set Dee style*
CHEEKS: *Jungle cock, drooping*

Clarence Gordon's old standard was the basis for this variation. I like to fish this pattern large, 4/0 and 5/0, for winter fish.

CUMMINGS, MARABOU

HOOK: *Low water or Bartleet style Spey hook*
TAG: *Flat silver tinsel*
BODY: *Rear third yellow floss; front two-thirds claret seal's fur or substitute*
RIB: *Flat silver tinsel with oval silver tinsel behind*
HACKLE: *Claret marabou over seal's fur behind ribs*
COLLAR: *Teal or gadwall flank feather, 1 1/2 turns*
WING: *Brown turkey tail or peacock secondary strips tied flat, Dee style*
CHEEKS: *Jungle cock, set low and drooping*

This is a variation of an old standard pattern that gives a better profile from all sides and a lot more movement. I began experimenting with marabou and converting traditional patterns to marabou Speys in 1990. Some old patterns lend themselves to this better than others.

POLAR SHRIMP, MARABOU

HOOK: *Bartleet style Spey hook or low water salmon, up to size 4/0 for winter use*
TAG: *Flat gold tinsel*
TAIL: *Dyed red golden pheasant crest*
BODY: *Rear third fluorescent hot orange floss; remainder hot orange seal's fur or substitute*
RIB: *Flat gold tinsel with oval or lace, three strand twist, behind*
HACKLE: *Hot orange marabou wrapped behind rib over seal's fur; strip one side of plume first; choose only fine stemmed feathers and tie them in by the tip, taking an additional turn or two at the shoulder before the collar is wound*
COLLAR: *Gadwall flank, 1 1/2 turns*
WING: *Two matching strips of goose shoulder or swan set flat and slightly splayed, Dee style or tented over Spey style*
CHEEKS: *Jungle cock, drooping with Dee wing and high with Spey wing*
HEAD: *Hot orange*

This is another marabou Spey conversion. I underwrap the body with flat tinsel. I like to fish these with a floating line year-round on a long leader. Two-handed Spey rods are ideal for this kind of fishing in winter.

PURPLE PERIL, MARABOU

HOOK: *Bartleet style Spey hook or large, up to 4/0, low water salmon hook*
TAG: *Flat silver tinsel*
TAIL: *Dyed purple golden pheasant crest*
BODY: *Rear third purple floss, remainder purple seal or substitute*
RIB: *Flat silver tinsel with oval silver tinsel behind; use gold tinsel for the rib and tag in low, clear water*
HACKLE: *Purple marabou over seal's fur behind ribs; strip one side and tie in by the tip*
COLLAR: *Gadwall flank, 1 1/2 turns*
WING: *Brown turkey tail or peacock secondary strips tied flat and splayed, Dee style*
CHEEKS: *Jungle cock, drooping*
HEAD: *Black*

An all-purple marabou gives a mobile bright, dark fly that is visible in most light conditions. This is my version of the old standard developed by Ken McLeod. I use some sort of Spey fly almost exclusively for my sunken fly presentation with marabou Spey/Dee flies virtually filling my fly box. Marabou gives movement unmatched by any feather, even heron. The color selection is quite broad, leaving a creative tier with many options. The durability can be increased by counter wrapping the stem with fine wire or burying the stem under the rib.

SKUNK, GREEN BUTT MARABOU

HOOK: *Bartleet style Spey hook or larger low water salmon hook for winter use*
TAG: *Flat silver tinsel partially covered with green floss*
TAIL: *Golden pheasant breast feather dyed red*
BUTT: *Black ostrich herl*
BODY: *Rear third black floss; remainder black seal's fur or substitute*
RIB: *Fine oval silver tinsel*
HACKLE: *Black marabou, one side stripped, tied in by the tip and wound behind ribs over seal's fur only*
COLLAR: *Gadwall flank, 1 1/2 turns*
WING: *Two white strips of goose shoulder or swan set flat, Dee style*
CHEEKS: *Jungle cock, drooping*

UMPQUA SPECIAL, MARABOU

HOOK: *Bartleet style Spey hook or larger low water salmon hook for winter use*
TAG: *Flat silver tinsel; continue as underbody*
TAIL: *White breast feather from an Amherst pheasant*
BODY: *Rear third yellow floss; remainder red seal's fur or substitute*
RIB: *Fine oval silver tinsel*
HACKLE: *Red marabou quill wound along rib, tied in by the tip, one side stripped, over seal's fur only*
COLLAR: *Widgeon flank feather, 1 1/2 turns*
WING: *Married strips of white and red swan or goose shoulder, white on each side of red, tied flat and splayed, Dee style*
CHEEKS: *Jungle cock, drooping*
HEAD: *Red*

Another marabou alternative to an old standard steelhead pattern. I have used a few of my own variations in this section to illustrate the possibilities when using standard patterns with nonstandard materials. An entirely new series of flies can be designed which may be more suitable for your fishing situation.

MAX CANYON SPEY

HOOK: *Alec Jackson Spey Hook, sizes 1 1/2-7*
TAG: *Fine oval silver tinsel*
BODY: *Rear two thirds hot orange floss; balance black seal's fur*
RIB: *Flat silver tinsel followed by small oval silver tinsel*
HACKLE: *Black Spey hackle over seal's fur only*
THROAT: *Additional turn of Spey hackle*
WINGS: *Four hot orange hackle tips set low*
CHEEKS: *California quail flank feathers (optional)*

Scott O'Donnell developed this version of the famous Deschutes River standard.

Plate 5 Page 76

MIDNIGHT BEAULY

HOOK: *Partridge low water N, size 1/0*
THREAD: *Black 6/0*
BODY: *Rear half flat pearl Mylar; front half black ostrich*
RIB: *Flat pearl Mylar over black ostrich*
HACKLE: *Gray marabou, one side stripped, tied in by the tip wound over the front half of the body, along ribs*
WING: *Black marabou*
COLLAR: *Hot pink SLF dubbed and picked out; SLF is a new synthetic dubbing from Partridge of England*

This is one of Mike Kinney's many patterns. The Midnight Beauly is a take-off on the Atlantic salmon pattern, Beauly Snow Fly.

MIDNIGHT CANYON

HOOK: *Bartleet or other salmon, sizes 2/0-2*
TAG: *Flat gold tinsel*
BODY: *Rear half flat silver tinsel; front half black seal's fur*
RIB: *Fine oval gold tinsel as a counter wrap after the hackle is applied*
HACKLE: *Black Spey hackle over tinsel; black and orange Spey hackle over seal's fur*
COLLAR: *Black Spey hackle or gadwall*
WING: *Black swan or goose shoulder with a narrow strip of orange on the bottom edge and a narrow strip of orange through the center; set low and tented over the body*
CHEEKS: *Jungle cock, tilted downward*
HEAD: *Black with a narrow band of orange*

This mobile dark Spey fly is a product of John Shewey and his creative mind.

NUMBER ONE

HOOK: *Bartleet or standard salmon, sizes 2/0-2*
THREAD: *Bright orange*
BODY: *Rear half flat silver tinsel; front half orange seal*
RIB: *Fine oval gold tinsel over seal only*
HACKLE: *Orange Spey hackle*
COLLAR: *Orange or flame red Spey hackle*
WING: *Hooded merganser flank feathers*
CHEEKS: *Jungle cock*
HEAD: *Orange*

This lovely bright Spey fly is another of John Shewey's unique Spey flies. The intense colors and large profile of this fly gives it good visibility from quite a distance.

ORANGE EAGLE

HOOK: *Bartleet or low water, up to 3/0 or 4/0*
THREAD: *Red*
TAG: *Fine oval silver tinsel*
TAIL: *Yellow golden pheasant rump feather*
BODY: *Flat silver tinsel*
RIB: *Large oval silver tinsel*
HACKLE: *Long orange marabou, several turns wound as a collar*
THROAT: *One or two turns of teal*
WING: *Peacock secondary wing strips*
HEAD: *Orange*

Joe Rossano of Seattle, Washington has adapted the Yellow Eagle, an old Atlantic salmon pattern, by using steelhead colors and a tinsel body.

ORANGE EGRET SPEY

HOOK: *Bartleet or standard salmon, sizes 2/0-4*
THREAD: *Bright orange*
TAG: *Flat silver tinsel, optional*
BODY: *Rear half orange silk floss; balance orange seal*
RIB: *Medium flat gold tinsel and a fine oval gold counter wrap*
HACKLE: *Light orange Spey hackle over seal*
COLLAR: *Bright orange Spey hackle*
WING: *Two bright orange hackle tips enveloping two flame red hackle tips*
HEAD: *Bright orange*

John Shewey, noted author and fly tier, developed his Orange Egret as a bright pattern with exceptional optical appeal.

ORANGE HERON (Burns)

HOOK: *Partridge Bartleet*
TAG: *Flat silver tinsel*
BODY: *Rear two-thirds light fluorescent orange floss; front third orange seal or substitute*
RIB: *Medium flat silver tinsel followed by fine oval silver tinsel*
HACKLE: *Gray heron substitute, from the second turn of tinsel*
COLLAR: *Cock de Leon*
WING: *Orange goose shoulder strips*
HEAD: *Orange*

This version of the Orange Heron was sent to me by David Burns of McCall, Idaho. David works with the Fisheries Department and ties Spey flies in his spare time.

ORANGE HERON (Glasso)

HOOK: *Low water salmon or Bartleet style Spey hook*
BODY: *Rear two-thirds orange floss; remaining one third orange seal's fur or substitute*
RIB: *Flat silver tinsel with oval silver tinsel behind it*
HACKLE: *Gray heron substitute, palmered along ribs*
THROAT: *Teal flank, sparse*
WING: *Four hot orange hackle tips, set low*
HEAD: *Red*

This is probably Syd Glasso's most recognized Spey fly. Many alternate dressings are around for this graceful fly yet this dressing still has a mystical attraction. It is very often the first Spey fly that many fishermen tie. Low water hooks, sizes 1 and 2, were used by Syd to tie his heron flies and I feel they look best.

ORANGE HERON (Gobin)

HOOK: *Alec Jackson Spey Hook with the eye straightened out*
EYE: *Silk gut or Dacron loop*
BODY: *Rear third fluorescent orange floss; remainder hot orange seal's fur*
RIB: *Medium flat silver tinsel and medium oval silver tinsel wrapped equidistant, counter wrapped over the hackle, with very fine oval silver tinsel*
HACKLE: *Black schlappen or heron substitute along ribs*
THROAT: *Teal flank, two turns*
WING: *Six narrow hot orange saddle hackle tips*
HEAD: *Red*

This is Steve Gobin's version of the Orange Heron. It varies little from the original, with the exception of the ribbing sequence and the hackle.

ORANGE HERON, JOHN'S (Shewey)

HOOK: *Partridge Bartleet or single salmon, sizes 2/0-2*
BODY: *Rear third orange floss; balance orange seal's fur*
RIB: *Wide flat gold tinsel followed by fine oval gold tinsel, counter wrap with fine gold to help reinforce the Spey hackle*
HACKLE: *Gray heron substitute along ribs over seal's fur only*
COLLAR: *Teal or pintail*
WING: *Bronze mallard strips set low*
HEAD: *Orange*

John Shewey of Aumsville, Oregon developed this version of the Orange Heron that he named John's Orange Heron. Heavier standard salmon hooks are used for winter or any deep, fast water.

ORANGE AND RED DEE

HOOK: *Partridge Bartleet, sizes 1/0-3/0, modified blind eye*
EYE: *20-pound Dacron loop eye*
THREAD: *Red 6/0*
TAG: *Flat silver tinsel*
TAIL: *Golden pheasant crest and tippet strands*
BODY: *Rear half medium orange seal's fur; front half scarlet red seal's fur*
RIB: *Medium oval silver tinsel*
HACKLE: *Medium orange saddle hackle over orange seal, dyed scarlet red pheasant rump over red seal*
COLLAR: *Teal or widgeon*
WING: *Cinnamon turkey tail strips, set Dee style*
CHEEKS: *Jungle cock, set low, drooping*
HEAD: *Red thread*

Greg Scot Hunt of Redmond, Washington sent this Dee Strip wing style fly. He finds it effective on winter steelhead. Much of Greg's work reflects the era of the classic salmon fly.

OSO MINT

HOOK: *Tiemco 7999, size 1/0*
THREAD: *Red 6/0*
BODY: *Rear half hot orange floss; front half hot orange polar bear dubbing*
TINSEL: *Wide, flat pearl Mylar*
HACKLE: *Fluorescent green marabou, tied in by the tip and stripped on one side, wound along the ribs*
COLLAR: *Teal*
WING: *Two pairs of golden pheasant breast feathers, the outside pair being somewhat shorter than the inner pair; tented over the body*

Mike Kinney of Oso, Washington developed this colorful pattern. Mike is a guide in the Skagit region and is known by many as "the old man of the river", although he is not old.

Plate 6 Page 77

POLAR SHRIMP (Glasso/Gobin)

HOOK: Alec Jackson Spey Hook with the eye straightened out
EYE: Silk gut or Dacron loop
BODY: Rear fourth orange floss; balance hot orange seal
RIB: Medium oval tinsel and medium flat gold tinsel wrapped equidistant; counter wrapped with extra fine oval silver tinsel
HACKLE: Deep reddish-orange Spey hackle
THROAT: Guinea hen
WING: Six matching white hackle tips set low or strips of white goose shoulder set low
HEAD: Red or black

Syd Glasso tied his own variation of the standard Polar Shrimp using his Spey fly technique. He fished this fly and his other Speys on the Olympic Peninsula near his home in Forks, Washington. Steve Gobin ties his version of Syd's pattern and also ties his light and dark versions of this classic fly.

POLAR SHRIMP, DARK (Gobin)

HOOK: Alec Jackson Spey Hook with the eye straightened out
EYE: Silk gut or Dacron loop
BODY: Hot orange seal or substitute, thin
RIB: Medium oval gold tinsel and medium flat silver tinsel wrapped equidistant; counter wrapped with extra fine oval silver tinsel
HACKLE: Hot orange Spey hackle
THROAT: Guinea hen
WING: Bronze mallard strips set low

Steve Gobin uses his Polar Shrimp patterns year-round with success in all his local rivers. To tie his Light version, substitute teal for the throat and bleached bronze mallard or white goose shoulder for the wings.

PSYCHEDELIC GREEN BUTT SKUNK

HOOK: Bartleet style Spey hook
TAG: Flat silver tinsel
TAIL: Dyed red golden pheasant crest
BODY: Rear half fluorescent green floss; front half black seal or substitute
RIB: Medium flat silver tinsel, followed by fine oval silver tinsel
HACKLE: Black hackle over seal
COLLAR: Natural blackish-green rump feather from a mallard
WING: Married strips of black and white goose shoulder; starting from the lower part of the wing: four black, one white, three black, two white, two black, three white, one black and four white
CHEEKS: Jungle cock
HEAD: Black

This is one of those patterns that doesn't fit a single category easily. It is tied along the lines of a Spey fly yet its body hackle is not long like most Spey patterns. David Burns of McCall, Idaho sent this to me.

PURPLE DEMON SPEY

HOOK: Bartleet style or low water salmon
BODY: Rear half flat silver tinsel; front half purple seal or substitute
RIB: Fine oval silver tinsel
HACKLE: Purple Spey hackle over seal
COLLAR: Hot orange guinea hen, long, 1 1/2 turns
WING: Four hot orange hackle tips set low
HEAD: Claret

PURPLE EAGLE

HOOK: Bartleet or low water, sizes up to 3/0 or 4/0
THREAD: Red
TAG: Fine oval silver tinsel
TAIL: Golden pheasant breast feather
BODY: Flat silver tinsel
RIB: Large oval silver tinsel
HACKLE: Purple marabou wound as a collar
THROAT: Teal
WING: Brown turkey strips
HEAD: Red

The Atlantic salmon influence is present in Joe Rossano's Purple Eagle. A variation on the theme of the 18th century Eagles used in the U.K., the Purple Eagle uses more suitable colors for winter steelhead.

QUILLAYUTE

HOOK: Low water salmon or Spey hook
TAG: Fine oval silver tinsel
TAIL: Golden pheasant breast feather fibers
BODY: Rear half fluorescent orange floss; remainder hot orange seal
RIB: Flat silver tinsel followed by fine oval silver tinsel
HACKLE: Teal flank or large gadwall flank feather palmered behind rib from second turn of tinsel
COLLAR: One turn of black heron or substitute
WING: Two pairs of red, golden pheasant breast feathers tented over the body
HEAD: Wine

This early steelhead Spey fly was originally designed by Dick Wentworth of Forks, Washington. Dick was a good friend and fishing partner of Syd Glasso. They were also fellow fly tiers. While Syd's influence is apparent in the design of the Quillayute, Dick Wentworth is a fine fly tier in his own right.

RADICAL DEPARTURE

HOOK: Alec Jackson Spey Hook, size 3, gold
THREAD: Black 6/0
BODY: Amethyst wool yarn
RIB: Flat pearl Mylar
HACKLE: Highlander green and purple schlappen, one side stripped, palmered along ribs
COLLAR: Pintail flank
WING: One pair of long golden pheasant breast feathers, enveloped by one shorter pair of purple pheasant rump feathers, enveloped by one even shorter pair of golden pheasant breast feathers

Mike Kinney of Oso, Washington developed this contrasting Spey pattern. Very few flies use the green and purple combination.

RAINBOW SPEY

HOOK: Daiichi J151
BODY: Embossed French silver tinsel, two layers, tinted with Magic Marker and coated with head cement; color blended from light to dark, butt to shoulder (see Rainbow Flies in the Wet Fly chapter)
RIB: Medium oval silver tinsel
HACKLE: Blue heron or substitute from the center of the body
COLLAR: Mallard flank dyed to match the color of the body
WING: Bronze mallard strips
HEAD: Colored with the same marker as the body

Mel Simpson has developed this style of body and uses it on his hairwing wet flies, featherwing wet flies and Spey flies. It allows for color and flash with a unique blending effect.

RED WING SPEY

HOOK: Alec Jackson Spey Hook, sizes 1 1/2-7
TAG: Fine oval silver tinsel
BODY: Rear two-thirds black floss; front third black ostrich herl
RIB: Fine oval silver tinsel
COLLAR: Long, webby black hen hackle
WING: Matching red goose shoulder strips (may substitute two pair of red hackle tips)
HEAD: Black

Brad Burden, the originator of the Red Wing Spey, says that a white-winged and black-winged version of this pattern are both effective variations.

Plate 7 Page 78

RICHIEHART

HOOK: Alec Jackson Spey Hook, sizes 1 1/2-7
BODY: Rear third purple floss or Antron fibers; remainder purple seal
RIB: Flat pearl Mylar, small or medium, with small oval tinsel behind
HACKLE: Dyed purple Spey hackle tied by the tip, wound behind ribs
THROAT: Blue peacock breast feather
WING: Four matching grizzly hackle tips dyed almost midnight blue; if you can't achieve this, try dying it dark blue

Dec Hogan feels his Richiehart, tied in various sizes and degrees of fullness, fills almost all of his fishing needs. It is named after his good friend and mentor, Charlie Gearhart, known as Richie Hart, professional musician and hardcore fly fisherman.

RIVER SPEY

HOOK: Alec Jackson Spey Hook or Bartleet
TAG: Fine oval gold tinsel
BODY: In four equal sections; mauve floss followed by mauve, bright purple and dark purple seal
RIB: Medium flat gold tinsel trailed by fine oval gold tinsel
HACKLE: Black Spey hackle over seal only
COLLAR: Lemon woodduck followed by long mauve schlappen
UNDERWING: Natural black squirrel tail
WING: Hooded merganser flank
CHEEKS: Jungle cock
HEAD: Red

I developed this pattern as a summer evening Spey fly. The violet tones work well in the fading light of summer twilight.

SANTIAM SPECTRUM SPEY

HOOK: Bartleet style or salmon, sizes 2/0-2
TAG: Silver tinsel, optional
BODY: Rear half flame red silk floss; front half purple seal
RIB: Medium flat silver tinsel; counter wrapped with fine, oval gold tinsel
HACKLE: Purple Spey hackle over seal only
COLLAR: Purple Spey hackle and teal flank
WING: Bronze mallard strips set low
CHEEKS: Jungle cock, optional
HEAD: Black or claret

The Santiam Spectrum is one of John Shewey's predominantly purple Spey flies. Anglers have begun to appreciate purple as a viable steelhead color and increase its application in their flies.

SILVER HERON

HOOK: Low water or Spey style salmon hook
BODY: Rear two-thirds flat silver tinsel; remainder black seal
RIB: Narrow oval silver tinsel
HACKLE: Gray heron, stripped on one side, palmered along ribs over black seal
COLLAR: Guinea, 1 to 1 1/2 turns
WING: Gray heron secondary wing strips or goose shoulder, set low and short

Another of Syd Glasso's Heron Spey flies he developed after the classic Spey fly of the 1800s. This dark Spey fly is a great summer pattern and an attractive fly.

SKYKOMISH DARK

HOOK: Alec Jackson Spey Hook with the eye straightened out
EYE: Silk gut or Dacron loop
BODY: Red seal or substitute, very thin
RIB: Medium oval silver tinsel and medium flat silver tinsel wrapped equidistant with an extra fine oval silver tinsel counter wrap
HACKLE: Yellow Spey hackle
THROAT: Golden pheasant breast feather
WING: Bronze mallard strips set low
HEAD: White

Steve Gobin devised this modification of the Skykomish Sunrise as a Spey fly. Steve, who resides in Marysville, Washington, is one of the most talented tiers in the Northwest.

SKYKOMISH LIGHT

HOOK: Alec Jackson Spey Hook with the eye straightened out
EYE: Silk gut or Dacron loop
BODY: Yellow seal or substitute
RIB: Medium oval silver tinsel and medium flat silver tinsel wrapped equidistant with a counter rib of extra fine oval silver tinsel
HACKLE: Yellow Spey hackle
THROAT: Golden pheasant breast feather
WING: Bleached bronze mallard strips set low
HEAD: White

This is the lighter version of Steve Gobin's Skykomish Spey. Not many steelhead flies use a predominantly yellow theme.

SKYKOMISH SPEY

HOOK: Alec Jackson Spey Hook, sizes 1 1/2-5, or Partridge N low water, sizes 1-3/0
TAG: Medium flat silver tinsel
TAIL: Dyed red golden pheasant crest
BODY: Rear two-thirds red floss; front third red seal or goat, thin and picked out
RIB: Fine oval silver tinsel
HACKLE: Long, dyed yellow Spey hackle over seal only
COLLAR: Dyed red guinea
WING: Married strips of yellow, white and red goose shoulder
CHEEKS: Jungle cock
HEAD: Red

Brad Burden developed this Spey alteration of the Skykomish Sunrise made famous by Ken and George McLeod in the 1940s. This graceful adaptation is fished in higher water on the larger Partridge low water hook.

SOL DUC

HOOK: Low water salmon or Bartleet style Spey hook
TAG: Flat silver tinsel
TAIL: Golden pheasant crest
BODY: Rear half fluorescent orange floss; balance hot orange seal
RIB: Flat silver tinsel
HACKLE: Long, webby yellow saddle hackle or schlappen, one side stripped, palmered along ribs starting at second turn
COLLAR: Teal flank, sparse
WING: Four hot orange hackle tips
TOPPING: Golden pheasant crest
HEAD: Wine

Syd Glasso's Sol Duc series is one of the most attractive set of flies around. They are striking in form and color and are very good fish catchers.

SOL DUC DARK

HOOK: Low water salmon or Spey style hook
TAG: Narrow oval silver tinsel
TAIL: Golden pheasant breast feather
BODY: Rear half fluorescent floss; remainder hot orange seal
RIB: Fine flat silver tinsel, followed by fine oval silver tinsel
HACKLE: Long, webby yellow saddle hackle or schlappen, one side stripped, starting behind second turn of tinsel
COLLAR: Teal flank, sparse, 1 to 1 1/2 turns only
WING: Four matching golden pheasant body feathers; breast feathers for smaller flies, flank feathers for larger flies
HEAD: Wine

A slightly darker version of Syd Glasso's Sol Duc.

SOL DUC SPEY

HOOK: Low water salmon or Bartleet style Spey hook
BODY: Rear half fluorescent orange floss; remainder hot orange seal
RIB: Flat silver tinsel
HACKLE: Long, webby yellow saddle hackle or schlappen, one side stripped, palmered along rib from second turn
COLLAR: Black heron substitute
WING: Four hot orange hackle tips
HEAD: Claret

This is one of Syd Glasso's Spey patterns developed for fishing the Sol Duc system. This graceful fly is part of the legacy that Mr. Glasso left us when he died in 1985.

Plate 8 Page 79

SOUTH FORK SALMON RIVER SPEY NO. 1

HOOK: *Alec Jackson Spey Hook*
TAG: *Fine oval silver tinsel, 2-5 turns*
BODY: *Rear third dark purple silk floss; balance thin black wool*
RIB: *No. 10 silver Mylar tinsel with very fine strip of hot pink Edgebright or hot pink floss over; followed with small oval silver tinsel and counter wrapped with fine silver wire after Spey hackle is wound*
HACKLE: *Blue eared pheasant dyed purple or purple marabou, one side stripped*
COLLAR: *Cock de Leon or teal*
WING: *Bronze mallard, tented Spey style*
HEAD: *Black*

This one of David Burns' favorite patterns for the Salmon River in Idaho. David Burns resides in McCall, Idaho and fishes very attractive flies.

SOUTH FORK SALMON RIVER SPEY NO. 2

HOOK: *Alec Jackson Spey Hook*
TAG: *Fine oval silver tinsel, 2-5 turns*
BODY: *Rear third bright claret seal; remainder dark purple seal*
RIB: *Medium flat silver tinsel followed by silver twist, counter wrapped with fine silver wire after Spey hackle is wound*
HACKLE: *Blue eared pheasant dyed black or black marabou; strip one side of either one; wrap behind ribs*
COLLAR: *Purple saddle*
WING: *Married goose shoulder strips from bottom to top: four strips purple, two strips red, one strip purple, two strips orange, one strip purple, two strips red and four strips purple; set low and tent over body*
HEAD: *Purple with blue sparkle nail polish over*

This is the second of David Burns' Spey fly series for the South Fork Salmon River in Idaho.

SOUTH FORK SALMON RIVER SPEY, FAVORITE VARMINT

HOOK: *Alec Jackson Spey Hook or Partridge Bartleet*
TAG: *Fine oval silver tinsel*
BODY: *Rear three-quarters purple floss; front quarter purple seal or substitute*
RIB: *No. 10 Mylar tinsel with a very narrow strip of hot pink Edgebright or floss overlaid on top; counter wrapped with fine oval silver tinsel*
HACKLE: *Dyed black blue eared pheasant, from second turn of tinsel*
COLLAR: *Guinea*
WING: *Bronze mallard*
HEAD: *Black*

The Favorite Varmint is David Burns' final entry of his Salmon River Spey series. Edgebright is a little hard to work with; floss may be an alternative.

SUBTLE EMERGENCE

HOOK: *Tiemco 7999, size 2/0*
THREAD: *Hot orange 6/0*
BODY: *Rear half hot orange floss; front half rusty-orange rabbit fur*
RIB: *Large oval silver tinsel*
HACKLE: *Golden pheasant tail section, stripped on one side and tied in by the butt, palmered along ribs*
COLLAR: *Unbarred natural woodduck flank feather*
WING: *Two pairs of natural ringneck pheasant rump feathers, the outer pair being about half the length of the inner pair*

Mike Kinney uses unusual materials in some of his Spey flies, pheasant tail for the Spey hackle is quite unique. The coloration of this pattern should make it useable during the October caddis season.

SUN FLY

HOOK: *Alec Jackson Spey Hook, sizes 3-7*
BODY: *Wide flat gold tinsel*
RIB: *Small oval gold tinsel*
HACKLE: *Dyed orange Chinese pheasant rump feather tied by tip and wound behind ribs*
THROAT: *Hot orange grizzly saddle*
WINGS: *Two orange hackle tips enveloped by two orange hackle tips*
CHEEKS: *Blue kingfisher*
HEAD: *Orange*

This is another of Dec Hogan's flies. This pattern, he says, is a good soft light pattern for summer midmornings, late fall and winter midday and shadowed waters on bright days.

SUNSET

HOOK: *Alec Jackson Spey Hook*
TAG: *Flat silver tinsel*
TAIL: *Dyed hot orange golden pheasant crest*
BUTT: *Black ostrich herl*
BODY: *Yellow floss*
RIB: *Fine oval silver tinsel*
HACKLE: *Dyed yellow Spey hackle; from the second turn of tinsel*
COLLAR: *Guinea hen*
WING: *Dark cerise goose shoulder strips set low*
CHEEKS: *Jungle cock*
HEAD: *Yellow*

The hues and tones of Joe Howell's Sunset truly remind you of an autumn sunset at the end of a warm, successful day on the river.

WHITE-WINGED AKROYD

HOOK: *Bartleet or low water style*
TAG: *Fine oval silver tinsel*
TAIL: *Golden pheasant crest and a few strands of tippet*
BODY: *Rear half yellow seal; front half black floss*
RIB: *Medium oval silver tinsel over both halves*
HACKLE: *Yellow saddle hackle over seal; black Spey hackle over the floss*
COLLAR: *Teal or gadwall*
WING: *White goose shoulder or swan strips, set Dee style*
CHEEKS: *Jungle cock, drooping*
HEAD: *Black*

This version of the legendary Akroyd was given to me by Joe Howell. The original Akroyd was a product of Charles Akroyd around 1878. Sometimes referred to as the "poor man's Jock Scott," this pattern was and is a very popular Atlantic salmon pattern and has found a faithful following among some steelheaders. Fishermen who use this pattern often fish it quite large, up to 4/0 and larger.

SUMMER VIOLET

HOOK: *Alec Jackson Spey Hook, size 3, gold*
THREAD: *Black 6/0*
TAG: *Medium round silver tinsel*
BODY: *Amethyst wool yarn*
RIB: *Wide flat pearl Mylar*
HACKLE: *Purple schlappen, one side stripped, palmered along ribs*
THROAT: *Deep gentian violet saddle and peacock breast*
WING: *Two pairs of purple pheasant rump feathers, the outside being about two-thirds the length of the inner pair*
TOPPING: *A few strands of peacock sword*

This striking pattern is one of Mike Kinney's many Spey flies. This pattern should do well in any low light condition or deep hole.

WHITE-WINGED PURPLE SPEY

HOOK: *Alec Jackson Spey Hook*
TAG: *Flat silver tinsel*
BODY: *Black floss*
RIB: *Fine oval silver tinsel*
HACKLE: *Purple Spey hackle, from the second turn of tinsel*
COLLAR: *Dyed blue guinea*
WING: *White strips of goose shoulder or swan, set in a traditional Spey style*
HEAD: *Black*

Joe Howell's White-winged Purple Spey is a dark pattern that has a good amount of colorful movement.

YELLOW JACKET

HOOK: *Alec Jackson Spey Hook, bronze, sizes 3-7*
BODY: *Rear fourth yellow floss; balance black seal*
RIB: *Small oval silver tinsel*
HACKLE: *Dyed yellow pheasant rump feather tied by tip, wound behind ribs*
THROAT: *Dyed yellow guinea*
WING: *Four black hackle tips*
HEAD: *Black*

The Yellow Jacket is a good gin clear water fly for summer and fall, says Dec Hogan, the originator.

Spey Flies Plate 1

Apple Maggot Spey (O'Donnell)

Autumn Skies No. 2 (Shewey)

Bedsprings Spey (Shewey)

Belvedere (Hogan)

Black Jack (Howell)

Brad's Brat Spey (Burden)

Brown Heron (Helvie)

Black Demon Spey (Helvie)

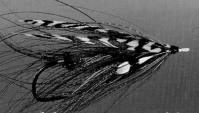

Caleb's Screamer (Helvie)

Carron Fly (Helvie)

Spey Flies Plate 2

Chappie Spey (Helvie)

Claret and Black Dee (Hunt)

Claret Spey (Gobin)

Deep Purple Spey (Gobin)

Deep Purple Spey (Helvie)

Blue Deependable (Rossano)

Gled Wing Deependable (Rossano)

Tartan Deependable (Rossano)

Dee's Demon (Shewey)

Desert Storm (Howell)

Spey Flies Plate 3

Dicos Spey (Helvie)

Double Eagle Spey (Shewey)

Fire Ant Spey (Burden)

Fire Plum Spey (Burden)

Floodtide Spey (Helvie)

Purple Floodtide Spey (Helvie)

Gold Heron (Helvie)

Golden Demon Spey (Burden)

Gray Heron (Helvie)

Hot Peacock Spey (Burden)

Jungle Cock Rock (Hogan)

Spey Flies Plate 4

Lady Caroline (Helvie)

Legal Eagle (Helvie)

McJones (Hogan)

Admiral Marabou (Helvie)

Black Gordon Marabou (Helvie)

Cummings Marabou (Helvie)

Polar Shrimp Marabou (Helvie)

Purple Peril Marabou (Helvie)

Green Butt Skunk Marabou (Helvie)

Umpqua Special Marabou (Helvie)

Max Canyon Spey (O'Donnell)

Spey Flies Plate 5

Midnight Beauly (Kinney)

Midnight Canyon (Shewey)

Number One (Shewey)

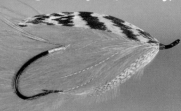

Orange Eagle (Rossano)

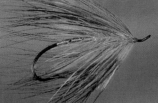

Orange Egret Spey (Shewey)

Orange Heron (Burns)

Orange Heron (Helvie)

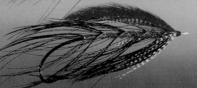

Orange Heron (Gobin)

John's Orange Heron (Shewey)

Orange and Red Dee (Hunt)

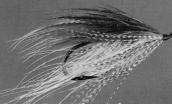

Oso Mint (Kinney)

Spey Flies Plate 6

Polar Shrimp, Glasso (Gobin)

Polar Shrimp, Dark (Gobin)

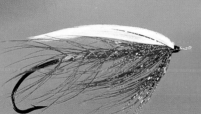

Polar Shrimp, Light (Gobin)

Psychedelic Green Butt Skunk (Burns)

Purple Demon Spey (Helvie)

Purple Eagle (Rossano)

Quillayute (Helvie)

Radical Departure (Kinney)

Rainbow Spey (Simpson)

Red Wing Spey (Burden)

Spey Flies Plate 7

Richiehart (Hogan)

River Spey (Helvie)

Santiam Spectrum Spey (Shewey)

Silver Heron (Helvie)

Skykomish Spey (Burden)

Skykomish, Dark (Gobin)

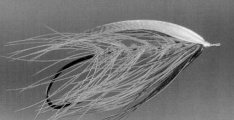

Skykomish, Light (Gobin)

Sol Duc (Helvie)

Sol Duc, Dark (Helvie)

Sol Duc Spey (Helvie)

Spey Flies Plate 8

South Fork Salmon River Spey No. 1 (Burns)

South Fork Salmon River Spey No. 2 (Burns)

South Fork Salmon River Spey, Favorite Varmint (Burns)   **Subtle Emergence (Kinney)**

Summer Violet (Kinney)

Sun Fly (Hogan)

Sunset (Howell)

White-Winged Ackroyd (Howell)

White-Winged Purple Spey (Howell)

Yellow Jacket (Hogan)

I HAVE RESERVED THIS CHAPTER FOR ALL PATTERNS meant to duplicate underwater food sources steelhead feed on in either their fresh water or salt water home. Some feel that virtually all flies imitate something and they are probably right.

Spey flies were first designed to represent shrimp which were a major food source for the Atlantic salmon of the River Spey, yet most of today's steelhead Spey flies are far from the Spey flies of the 1800s.

Dry fly fishermen remind us that most of their flies are also designed to look like many of the surface bugs that steelhead feed on during their trip back home. What I am referring to are the prawn and shrimp patterns that are becoming popular with a growing group of steelhead fishermen. Other flies in this category are the various nymphs and leech patterns that are so often fished deep and slow for both summer and winter fish.

I concede that there are other patterns that do a fairly good job of representing one of the steelhead's many food groups but I feel this chapter should be reserved for those nontraditional wet patterns that leave the viewer with a definite idea of what the fly is meant to represent.

When Colonel Esmond Drury sat down to design his General Practitioner in 1953, he did it almost out of spite. Earlier that season, the use of real prawns was outlawed on one of his favorite stretches of river and the Colonel wanted a pattern that would help him overcome the new regulation. His new fly was almost as effective as nature's original. From his creation, many off-shoots have evolved. The colors range from chartreuse to black and the sizes include patterns as large as 8/0.

Nymphs, especially the stonefly nymph, prove to be a good pattern throughout the season, accounting for many fish each year. Steelhead fishermen fish the stonefly nymph much like trout fishermen with a floating line and often a strike indicator. Black and brown are the predominant colors of most stonefly nymphs but other colors do show up from time to time.

Winter fishing brings out the leeches. Not real ones, mainly bunny strip leeches that are dredged along the bottom of the river to entice big steelhead to strike. As ugly as they may be, these unclassy flies catch a lot of fish. Dark colors, black, purple and blue are good in the low light conditions of winter.

Most Imitator patterns are either self-explanatory or seem to fall into the General Practitioner style of tying, so this will be the only fly in the "how to" section of this chapter. The pattern I use is a variation called the Pheasant General Practitioner. Color variations include orange, red, pink, purple and black, I will tie a red one.

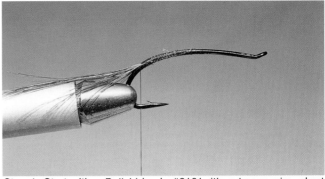

Step 1: Start with a Daiichi hook, #2161, it's a heavy wire, short shanked Bartleet style hook, I use sizes 1 and 2. Because the fly is not large, it makes a good summer and fall dressing. To this attach your thread, red unwaxed 6/0, and bring to rear, into the bend slightly. Tie in some long fibers from a dyed red golden pheasant rump feather, these are the feelers.

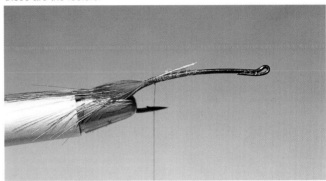

Step 2: Tie in a small, dyed red pheasant breast feather over about a third of the tail, curving downward, this is the head.

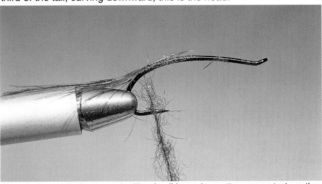

Step 3: Separate the thread with a bodkin and wax the separated section or loop. Insert red seal or goat fur in thread and spin the bobbin to tighten the dubbing, about two inches of dubbed thread should be sufficient.

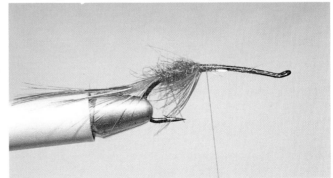

Step 4: Wind your dubbed thread forward about a third of the body length. The dubbing should end there. Tie in a small dyed red flank feather by the tip, fold it and wind a couple of turns. Trim the fibers off the very top of the hackle.

Step 5: At this point tie in a dyed red golden pheasant breast feather. This should be tied flat and extend just beyond the bend of the hook.

Step 6 & 7: Over the breast feather, tie in a dyed red tippet feather with the center cut out. I put a thin coat of cement on the tippet to stiffen it. Tie in the feather flat.

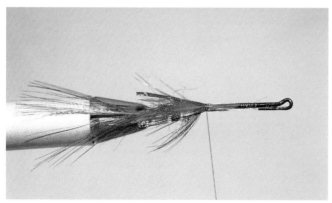

Step 8: Again, separate the thread, wax it and dub a small amount of red seal or goat. Wind it forward another third of the way and tie in another slightly longer red rump feather and take a couple of turns.

Step 9: Tie in another red breast feather extending back enough to cover the previous shellback, or breast feather, about half way.

Step 10: Dub the final section the same way as before. Tie in a slightly longer red flank feather than the middle one and fold it and take a couple of turns.

Step 11: Tie in the final shellback of a red breast feather, this one should be as long, or slightly longer, than the second. Finish off the head and the fly is completed.

If you experience trouble with the shellbacks rolling, flatten the stems with a small pair of flat pliers. I, personally, like to pick the body out fairly shaggy for the living look. This pattern has no rib and the hackle is not palmered so it is faster to tie than the original General Practitioner.

Plate 1 Page 86

BUNNY LEECH

HOOK: *Standard salmon or long shanked streamer hook, sizes 6 and larger, I prefer the Daiichi J141*
TAIL: *Straight cut rabbit strip about the length of the shank, topped with a few strands of Krystal Flash or Flashabou*
BODY: *Crosscut rabbit strip palmered over the body sweeping back*
EYES: *Lead or brass barbell eyes, optional*

This generic leech pattern is a good fish catcher tied in black and purple. The tail and body are usually tied the same color. Although these patterns are not graceful by any means they *do* catch fish. When wet these flies remind a person of casting with road kill on the end of the line. These patterns are probably responsible for the "Chuck and Duck" method of casting.

DARK STONE NYMPH

HOOK: *2-3X long nymph hook or Partridge Draper nymph hook, sizes 2-6*
TAIL: *Dark brown goose biots, two*
ABDOMEN: *Brown Swannundaze over a tapered underbody of lead wire and floss*
THORAX: *Dark brown rabbit dubbing*
LEGS: *Grouse hackle feather separated into three pairs of legs and coated with head cement to stiffen. These go over the thorax and under the shellback*
SHELLBACK: *Black Swiss Straw*
FEELERS: *Dark brown goose biot fibers*
HEAD: *Dark brown rabbit dubbing*

This is my generic stonefly nymph which I use for steelhead and trout. Change the color and size for the various species found throughout the West and you have a very effective fly.

FIRE TAILED LEECH

HOOK: *Daiichi Bob Johns winter run, J141, sizes 1 and 2*
TAIL: *Straight cut rabbit strip with a small piece of hot pink or hot orange rabbit strip cemented on the end, skin to skin*
BODY: *Crosscut rabbit strip wound from tail to head*
EYES: *Bead chain or brass barbell eyes, optional*

I generally tie this pattern with black or purple as the base color and the fire tail of either pink or orange. Other colors, blues and reds work well in certain water conditions. Chartreuse is also a good tail color with the black body.

GENERAL PRACTITIONER

HOOK: *Tier's choice, Partridge N low water is my preference. Bartleet style hooks tie an attractive fly but I feel this lighter wire hook helps the fly to roll over and fish upside down. If you don't have an ethical problem with them, low water double hooks swim these flies well and sink well on a floating line. I use the Daiichi 2161 in sizes 1 and 2 for my summer G.P.'s. This hook is slightly shorter and the heavier wire helps it swim well*
THREAD: *Orange*
TAIL: *Small bunch, 12 or so, orange polar bear hair or bucktail. The tail should be fairly long, about the length of the body or longer*
HEAD: *Two matching red golden pheasant breast feathers, the bottom one shiny side down and the top one shiny side up*
BODY: *Three sections of orange seal or goat dubbing.*
RIB: *Fine oval gold tinsel (often omitted)*
HACKLE: *Orange neck hackle palmered along ribs, tapering larger at the rear and smaller at the eye of the hook. The hackle will have to be tied in three separate sections*
SHELLBACKS: *Natural red golden pheasant breast feathers. Tie in one, flat, over each body section after the body section and hackle are applied*
EYES: *Natural golden pheasant tippet cut into a "V" and tied in after the first section and pointing towards the rear with the tip of the feather just past the bend of the hook*

The General Practitioner is dressed differently by almost every tier. This is the way I tie a full-dressed G.P. Some reference books show this fly as tied on small hooks originally, while others show this fly first tied on the old-style long Dee or Double Dee hooks used for some of the classic Dee Strip Wing patterns. The only sample of this fly I have seen tied by Esmund Drury, its originator, was tied on a small, size two, single salmon hook.

The fact that this pattern has spawned so many variations says something for it, especially since it is an Atlantic salmon pattern. Yet success cannot be measured by how a pattern started but how it has had an overall effect on the steelhead fly fisherman. True to the form of a real shrimp or prawn, the hackle should be longer towards the bend of the hook and shorter towards the eye although many tiers feel it is more pleasing to the fisherman's eye to have the hackle shorter at the bend.

While the General Practitioner is not what most tiers call a classic salmon fly, because of the era and the style, it really does have a tremendous amount of historical appeal. A well-tied Practitioner is a very attractive and functional pattern that some tiers may find to be a good pattern to perfect. It can test a tiers sense of proportion and creativeness when it comes to color selection.

Although orange is the original color, variations on the color scheme abound. Deep and bright red, cerise, purple, black and combinations such as orange and cerise are found in many fishermen's fly boxes.

HOLST'S STONEFLY NYMPH

HOOK: *Mustad 9672 or equivalent, sizes 2-6*
TAIL: *Two white rubber hackle fibers, splayed and long*
ABDOMEN: *Black chenille*
THORAX: *Fluorescent green chenille*
HACKLE: *Three turns of black hackle through the thorax*
SHELLBACK: *Two or three strands of black chenille pulled over the thorax*
FEELERS: *Two white rubber hackle fibers, splayed and long*

Bryan Holst of Roseburg, Oregon ties this bright nymph pattern for summer or winter fish. Weighted and fished deep on a floating line, patterns like this do well in summer and winter when water conditions permit.

K. F. SHRIMP

HOOK: *Extra heavy wire English style bait hook, preferably the discontinued Tiemco 207BL, Gamakatsu also makes a comparable hook, sizes 2-4*

THREAD: *Hot green*

UNDERBODY: *Lead wire if extra weight is desired*

TAIL: *Fluorescent green Krystal Flash*

ABDOMEN: *Hot green Antron yarn*

RIB: *Single strand fluorescent green floss over abdomen only, after shellback is pulled over*

SHELLBACK: *Fluorescent green Krystal Flash over both abdomen and thorax, about 20-25 strands.*

THORAX: *Fluorescent green chenille*

LEGS: *A few strands of fluorescent green Krystal Flash tied in after each wrap of chenille getting longer towards head*

FEELERS: *Four strands of flourescent green Krystal Flash twice as long as the rest of the fly*

EYES: *Extra small black mono eyes*

The abdomen is about 2/3 the length of the body. The shellback is pulled over the abdomen, tied off and ribbed and trimmed off. Then tie in another bunch of Krystal Flash for the shellback over the thorax.

I designed this fly for fishing on a floating fly line for winter steelhead, I find that a dead drift with this fly gives a much more natural presentation. Other color combinations for this fly are hot orange, fluorescent pink and white with shell pink Krystal Flash.

Plate 2 Page 87

OSTRICH HERL G.P.

HOOK: *Partridge N low water hook, sizes 1/0-3/0*

THREAD: *Orange*

TAIL: *Dyed orange polar bear, approximately the length of the body*

HEAD: *Natural red golden pheasant breast feather*

BODY: *Alternate bands of dyed ostrich herl (The body is built to have three sections, each "section" consists of two bands, or balls, of herl)*

HACKLE: *Dyed orange hen hackle, folded, 1 1/2 turns at each herl band or ball. The hackle should be tapered with the largest towards the rear of the hook and the smallest towards the eye, do not palmer the hackle over the whole body*

RIB: *None*

SHELLBACK: *Natural red golden pheasant breast feathers, one at the first section and the second section and two matching longer ones covering the other shellbacks tied in at the head*

EYES: *Dyed orange golden pheasant tippet cut into a "V" and tied in on top of the first shellback*

Brad Burden's version of the General Practitioner is another example of utilizing materials to help a pattern fit your fishing situation. The ostrich herl body absorbs water and helps the fly to remain sunk on the swing, according to Brad. The herl also gives movement to the fly that some "more traditional" materials don't.

After carefully examining the fly sent to me by Brad, I tried to describe its tying process as best I could, hopefully with adequate clarity. The colors don't have to be orange only, red and purple on this fly work well.

SAUK RIVER GRUB

HOOK: *Alec Jackson Spey Hook or Partridge low water hook for larger sizes, 1/0 and up*

BODY: *Three to five "balls" of twisted ostrich herl chenille*

COLLAR: *At the joint of each "ball", a full turn of hackle getting larger from rear to front*

NOTE: The colors of the body and hackles are generally of red and orange tones. Judging from the samples sent to me by Alec, the colors can be quite varied. By adding a tail of long bucktail or, as in the sample, guinea fibers the Sauk River Grub becomes the Sauk River Shrimp.

Alec Jackson developed these two flies as his larger, winter attractor patterns. Again, Alec utilizes his method of using ostrich herl twisted with tinsel for his bodies, even on shrimp and grub patterns.

When many of us sit down at our fly tying bench and create something we then wonder if it will catch fish. Alec Jackson appears to tie with a mission, design a fly for a situation. We all can learn from Alec's approach to tying and fishing. The purpose of these two patterns is to get good presentation along with the illusion of bulk without heavy underwraps of lead. They accomplish both. Tied on heavy hooks, Partridge M or N salmon irons, these flies will sink quite well on a floating line and the ostrich gives the appearance of bulk.

SIMPLE SCHRIMP

HOOK: *Tiemco standard salmon, sizes 8 to 2/0*

THREAD: *Shell pink 6/0 flymaster*

TAIL: *A few strands each of peccary and polar bear hair, about 1 1/2 times the length of the body topped with a golden pheasant tippet with the center removed to make a "V"-shaped section, topped with a hackle tip*

EYES: *Map pins dipped in black lacquer*

BODY: *Flat silver metallic tinsel as an underbody with orange seal fur or substitute dubbed loosely as to let the tinsel "glow" through*

HACKLE: *Webby, magenta, Chinese saddle hackle palmered over the body*

RIB: *Oval gold tinsel to reinforce the hackle, optional*

WING: *A small bunch of pink marabou topped with three or four strands of pearl Krystal Flash, topped with another small bunch of marabou, orange, then tie in two matching fire red hackle tips on top of the other*

COLLAR: *Reddish golden pheasant flank feather folded and wound over the wing butts*

This schrimp pattern was sent to me by Stephen Gill. As with most shrimp patterns, the tail is actually the head and feelers. Stephen gives a few helpful hints when tying and fishing this fly. Before the eyes are tied in, bend them up 30 degrees about a quarter inch from the eye. He feels that the hook, tinsel and eyes are all the weight this fly needs and fishes it on a floating line. When more weight is needed he used a Sue Burgess weighted, titanium, braided salmon leader which is easily removed. When the water is supposedly out of shape, he fishes it tight to the bank and will also use it on a greased line but will tie it without the tinsel underbody. The sample described is the red version, he also ties pink, chartreuse, black and purple, also shown in the plate.

TRAGOPRAWN

HOOK: *Partridge N low water or Bartleet, sizes up to 3/0*

THREAD: *Orange*

TAIL OR FEELERS: *Very sparse, 8-12, dyed orange polar bear hairs, 1 1/2 times as long as hook*

HEAD: *Red pheasant breast feather over the tail fibers, 1/4 to 1/5 as long*

BODY: *Four sections of hot orange seal or polar bear dubbing*

RIB: *Fine oval gold tinsel*

HACKLE OR LEGS: *One turn of dyed orange guinea at the joint of each section and after the last section as a beard, hackles should be tapered from large to small towards the eye of the hook*

EYES: *Stamens or dressmaker pins painted silver/gray and varnished tied in after the first body section, stamens are found in a craft shop or florist shop***SHELLBACKS**: *Four breast feathers from a red tragopan pheasant tied in after each section of the body is applied, curving over the back of the fly. The feather used is the rusty-orange feather with a large gray dot in the center*

HEAD: *One turn of orange seal*

Dec Hogan's exotic version of the General Practitioner utilizes the somewhat rare tragopan or red pheasant.

WADDINGTON WABBIT

HOOK: *A Waddington shank and a short single salmon hook, such as the Tiemco 800B, sizes 1-2. Stiffen the connection by tying a section of stiff mono between the two*

TAIL: *A small bunch of pink or cerise Flashabou topped with a short piece of black rabbit strip*

BODY: *Black rabbit strip wound on the hook and on the Waddington shank the full length of the shank*

Doug Nelson gave me his jumbo bunny leech and tells me he ties it in black and purple. He uses 45 and 35 millimeter shanks, the shank really doesn't need to be weighted.

WINTER PRAWN

HOOK: *Partridge N low water sizes as large as you want to cast*

FEELERS: *Two stiff guard hairs from the back of a javelina, 1 1/2 times as long as the hook*

HEAD: *One natural ringneck hip feather topped with a dyed black hip feather slightly shorter. I say hip feather because I don't want you to think of the long, webby rump feather. Hip feathers are heart-shaped small feathers just above the rump feathers*

BODY: *Three sections of a blend of black and olive polar bear dubbing or seal fur picked out and shaggy*

RIB: *Fine copper wire*

HACKLE OR LEGS: *One turn at each body joint of dyed black pheasant rump feather, longer at the rear of the hook, tapered to the eye. Do not palmer the hackle over the entire body*

EYES: *Jungle cock tied in after the first body joint, horizontally and covering the first body joint*

SHELLBACK: *Tied in after each body joint, one natural ringneck hip feather partially covered by a dyed black hip feather as the head is done*

This truly wicked looking prawn is a product of the fertile mind of Dec Hogan. Dec is an avid fisherman and guide from Mt. Vernon, Washington. Generally, Dec fishes this in sizes 1/0-3/0, smaller gets hard to tie and larger gets hard to cast. Fish it deep and slow!

Imitators Plate 1

Bunny Leech (Helvie)

Dark Stone Nymph (Helvie)

Fire Tailed Leech (Helvie)

General Practitioner (Helvie)

General Practitioner, Red (Helvie)

General Practitioner, Purple (Helvie)

Holst's Stonefly Nymph (Holst)

K.F. Shrimp (Helvie)

Imitators Plate 2

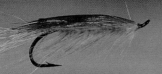

Ostrich Herl G.P. (Burden)

Sauk River Grub (Jackson)

Sauk River Shrimp (Jackson)

Simple Schrimp, Red (Gill)

Simple Schrimp, Orange (Gill)

Simple Schrimp, Green (Gill)

Simple Schrimp, Purple (Gill)

Simple Schrimp, Black (Gill)

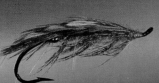

Tragoprawn (Hogan)

Winter Prawn (Hogan)

Waddington Wabbit (Nelson)

Very few things are as exciting as a big, fresh steelhead exploding onto a well-presented dry fly. Whether the fly is a traditional dry fly or a skater or a waking dry fly the thrill is the same. Many of the Pacific Northwest's rivers have become more fishable with the dry fly over the past few years with warmer temperatures and lower water levels. Speaking from personal experience, the summer of 1992 started off as dry fly water on the North Umpqua. I raised my first steelhead on a dry on Memorial Day, the earliest I have ever raised a fish to a dry on the North Umpqua. Granted, that steelhead was raised while trout fishing with a golden stonefly pattern but it was a steelhead nonetheless.

Some rivers are more accessible than others to the dry fly fisherman. Sometimes it's because the water conditions present themselves better or possibly the fish strain in that river react better to flies presented on the surface. Some fishermen on British Columbia rivers have had success with surface bugs in cold water temperatures where I would not even attempt to fish dries on the North Umpqua.

Summer fishing is a different story on most rivers. The summer steelhead runs on most rivers can be fished on the surface at some time during the season. Insects of various types are hatching throughout most of the warm weather. The stonefly and its cousin the salmonfly, along with the numerous caddis flies capping off with the giant October caddis in late summer and fall, provide a good food source for hungry steelhead. Throughout the summer months some rivers may have other forms of aquatic insects that steelhead feed on freely.

Not all surface flies are actually on the surface, many are fished in the surface film or just under it. Nor are all surface flies meant to imitate an insect. Many surface flies are fished damp, this allows the fly to work the top of the water naturally by struggling in and out of the surface film, just as a real insect might do while fighting the current to the top. Often movement, and not necessarily color, is the most important thing. Movement while fishing the surface is a very important facet in the success of the fly. Many of the surface flies sent to me were tied with natural, undyed, deer, elk and moose hair. These flies catch fish even though they don't match any particular color of insect at the time. Their movement is what attracts fish, with the erratic action these bugs provide color becomes a less dominant factor.

The selection of the water you fish a dry fly in will, of course, have a lot to do with the success of the dry fly fisherman. Nothing is impossible when fishing but the success rate of pulling a winter steelhead from twenty feet down and then up to the surface is pretty low. If a fisherman is to fish dries with good results on a regular basis he must be more selective on the water he is going to fish. Fishing a lie that is six to eight feet deep with a surface bug is a more realistic feat than fishing the same fly over that fish in twenty feet of water.

The hooks for the steelhead dry are most often a lighter wire which helps the floatability of the fly. Most manufacturers of hooks provide the tier with a model or two that will. Low water hooks are generally light enough to do the job and will be a little stronger than a traditional salmon dry fly hook. The Partridge Bartleet in smaller sizes and the Alec Jackson Spey Hook work well for many of the surface or damp patterns.

When tying surface flies for steelhead, material selection is important even though many of today's popular styles of surface fly don't require good quality dry fly hackle to tie. Very often these flies are tied solely with deer, elk or moose hair and require no hackle at all. Yet when tying standard dry fly steelhead patterns, Wulff's and Bivisibles for example, good dry fly hackle is important although it is very hard to find dry fly hackle large enough to tie size 2 and 4 flies.

Spinning hairs, such as deer, elk and moose are becoming the norm on steelhead dry flies because of the buoyancy of these materials. Bombers and other flies with spun hair for the bodies work well in Western rivers where the water is much rougher than the pristine limestone creeks of the East.

Patterns abound that use hair to form the body without spinning the hair. Attaching the hair lengthwise, by binding the hair down with thread, to make the body offers the fisherman a sleeker body, with less bulk, without sacrificing the buoyancy of the bug.

What I consider a dry fly may not be what other fishermen deem as such. For the sake of continuity in this class of dry fly I am going to include damp flies. I do this because the damp fly on the tail of a drift often becomes dry just before the take. Very often the classic dry fly will drown midway through a swing and is often keyed on by a steelhead at this moment.

Steelheading with surface flies is the most rewarding and pleasurable way to fish, for me. It provides the most control of my fly and travels on the drift, the fish's take is always exciting.

Plate 1 Page 92

AUTUMN LINER

HOOK: *Partridge Wilson dry 01, sizes 10-2*
THREAD: *Tan 6/0*
TAG: *Small oval silver tinsel*
TAIL: *Blonde elk*
BODY: *Dubbed seal's fur or substitute, in equal parts blending from golden brown to reddish-brown to dark brown*
RIB: *Small oval silver tinsel*
THROAT: *Dark Hungarian partridge*
UNDERWING: *Dark mottled brown turkey*
WING: *Dark elk topped with light elk*
HEAD: *Leave the butts of the light elk and trim to about 1/8" long and cement with a couple of coats then flatten them, pointing upward about 45 degrees*

Jim Birrell of Seattle, Washington sent me this takeoff of the Greased Liner. Jim stresses that the head should be stiff to give this fly a "lively fashion". Recement the head after fishing if needed.

BEETLE BUG

HOOK: *Salmon or steelhead dry*
TAIL: *Stiff brown moose hair*
BODY: *Red floss*
WING: *White bucktail, upright and divided*
HACKLE: *Reddish brown saddle hackle, full*
HEAD: *Black*

This is an older dry fly pattern that has proven productive for quite a few years. The originator of this pattern escapes me but its design is similar to the Wulff series.

BOMBER

HOOK: Standard salmon dry fly hook.
TAIL: Fine, dark squirrel tail, pine squirrel is my choice
WING: The same as the tail, pointing forward over the eye of the hook
BODY: Deer body hair, spun and clipped like a fat cigar
HACKLE: Grizzly, or other colored, hackle. I chose black for the sample, palmered over the body

The basic Bomber pattern has been a catalyst for many dry fly developments in the steelheader's world. Because of its body material this fly, and others like it, float very well. After its introduction to Atlantic salmon in the 1960s, the Bomber made its way west and the steelhead fishermen grabbed it up.

ENTERPRISE

HOOK: Partridge Wilson Dry or any standard dry salmon iron, sizes 4-6. Bend the hook up slightly to get the skating effect desired, "fluttering like a bird trying to get off the water"
THREAD: Brown monocord
TAIL AND BODY: Stiff mule deer hair, the tail is an extension of the body and is ribbed both back and forth with the tying thread
WINGS: Stiff moose hair out to the side and back
HEAD: Spun deer hair flattened out to a disc shape and coated with a stiff cement or aqua seal, trim all around about the size of a dime

Eric Pettine is a dentist from Fort Collins, Colorado who loves to fish for steelhead with a dry fly whenever he can. The Enterprise is his fly which has proven effective on the Babine and Kispiox Rivers with fish to almost twenty pounds. While showing it to a fellow Colorado steelheader, Al Makkai, at Smithers B.C., he was told it looked like the "Starship Enterprise", hence the name.

GRIZZLY WULFF

HOOK: Salmon dry fly hook
THREAD: Black
TAIL: Brown bucktail
BODY: Yellow floss
WING: Brown bucktail, upright and divided
HACKLE: Brown and grizzly saddle hackle, full
HEAD: Black

This is one of Lee Wulff's patterns which has become a very popular pattern for summer steelhead. I have found it effective, because of its body color, when grasshoppers are on the prowl.

MACINTOSH

HOOK: Salmon dry fly hook
BODY: None
WING: Natural brown bucktail or fox squirrel tail attached to the center of the hook, horizontally, about a full hook length past the bend of the hook
HACKLE: Three or four brown saddle hackles wound full, starting at the center of the hook

This simple pattern is an Atlantic salmon pattern gone west. With the stiff wing/tail and heavy hackle, this pattern stays on the surface well. The MacIntosh also works on a dead drift and will skate without a lot of trouble.

ON FIRE LINER

HOOK: Partridge Wilson dry 01, sizes 10-2
THREAD: Red 6/0
TAG: Small oval silver tinsel
TAIL: Dark brown to black elk
BODY: Dubbed seal fur or substitute, rear 1/4 red and the balance black
RIB: Small oval silver tinsel
THROAT: Teal flank
UNDERWING: Two golden pheasant breast feathers dyed hot orange tied in a bunch to the center of the tail
WING: Dark brown or black elk
SIDES: Golden pheasant neck feathers
HEAD: Trim butts of elk to about 1/8" and flair upward 45 degrees and flatten. Liberally apply a couple of coats of cement to stiffen

Another of Jim Birrell's surface patterns that he insists must be fished with a lot of movement.

ROYAL WULFF

HOOK: Salmon dry fly hook
TAIL: Stiff, medium brown moose hair
BODY: Peacock herl with a red floss center joint
WING: White or natural brown bucktail, upright and divided
HACKLE: Stiff, reddish-brown (Royal Coachman Brown) saddle hackle, full
HEAD: Black

Lee Wulff introduced the Royal Wulff, one of his Wulff series, as a substitute for the Royal Coachman. With its fuller hackle and hair tail and wing it is better suited for West coast steelhead rivers.

RUSTY POPPER

HOOK: Partridge Wilson 01, sizes 10-2
THREAD: Black 6/0
TAG: Small, flat gold tinsel
TAIL: Dark brown or black elk
BODY: Medium, flat gold tinsel
RIB: Small, oval silver tinsel
UNDERWING: Dark brown mottled turkey
WING: Reddish pheasant feathers, tragopan
COLLAR: Dyed rust deer hair spun to the center off the wing
HEAD: Dyed rust deer hair spun and trimmed evenly to a tapered cone, roughly one quarter of the body length. Liberally apply two coats of cement to the face of the head and flatten, allowing to dry with ridges

Jim Birrell developed this muddler variation. He fishes it on a riffling hitch, in a downstream direction, stressing that it must be fished with movement.

Plate 2 Page 93

SEAL SKATER, BLACK

HOOK: Light wire salmon dry or Bartleet, sizes 4-10
TAG: Flat silver tinsel with fluorescent green floss covering 3/4 of the tinsel
TAIL: Stiff, dark brown to black moose hair, fairly long
BODY: Black seal
RIB: Fine oval silver tinsel
WING: Stiff, dark brown to black moose, set forward and divided
THROAT: Four strands each of black and pearl Krystal Flash
COLLAR: Soft black or grizzly hen hackle, two turns behind wings, two turns in front of wings

SEAL SKATER, PURPLE

HOOK: *Fine wire salmon dry or Bartleet, sizes 4-10*
TAG: *Flat silver tinsel with fluorescent orange floss covering 3/4 of the tinsel*
TAIL: *Light brown or gray stiff moose, fairly long*
BODY: *Purple seal*
RIB: *Fine oval silver tinsel*
WING: *Light brown or gray stiff moose, set forward and divided*
THROAT: *Four strands each of hot orange and dark purple Krystal Flash*
COLLAR: *Deep purple hen hackle, two turns behind wings and two turns in front of wings*

I developed these two skaters as evening patterns. Fished quartered downstream and on a riffling hitch, these flies skate very well. When tying these flies I tie in the tail and the wing before the body is applied, saturate the wing butts with cement to stiffen them even more.

SOFT WATER SEDGE

HOOK: *Partridge Wilson dry 01, sizes 8-10*
THREAD: *Black 6/0*
BODY: *Loosely dubbed seal fur, rear half gold; front half gold brown*
RIB: *Fine oval silver tinsel*
HACKLE: *10 to 12 black moose mane hairs, twice the body length*
WING: *Two red, dotted tragopan pheasant feathers tented over body, topped with two, smaller, Mearns quail feathers. Mottled pheasant body feathers can be substituted for the hard to find Mearns quail*
HEAD: *Spin a small head of rust deer hair and pull it back over body and wings and trim into a ragged, bullet head*

This buggy pattern is the product of Jim Birrell's creative mind. Body color can be altered to fit local hatches of caddis. This is a great looking bug!

SOLDIER PALMER

HOOK: *Salmon dry fly hook*
THREAD: *Black*
TAIL: *Dark ginger hackle fibers*
BODY: *Red floss*
RIB: *Fine oval gold tinsel and palmered with a dark ginger saddle hackle*
HACKLE: *Four dark ginger saddle hackles, full*
HEAD: *Black*

Another trout/Atlantic salmon pattern which has worked well for a traditional dry fly presentation.

SPEED SKATER, BROWN/GRIZZLY

HOOK: *Dry fly salmon hook*
TAIL: *Brown elk or deer, stiff*
BODY: *Grizzly cock neck hackle wound tight over the rear half or two thirds of the hook*
WING/HACKLE: *Natural deer hair spun and flared out to form a hackle*

SPEED SKATER, DARK

HOOK: *Dry fly salmon hook*
TAIL: *Moose mane*
BODY: *Furnace cock neck hackle wound tight over the rear half of the hook*
WING: *Black deer hair spun and flared out to form a hackle*

A hard pattern to describe, Joe Rossano's skater is a takeoff on the Bivisible design. With the deer hairwing/collar, this pattern is hard to sink.

STEELHEAD BEE

HOOK: *Salmon dry*
TAIL: *Red squirrel tail*
BODY: *Seal or substitute in three equal sections; brown, yellow and brown, the body should be buggy*
WING: *Red squirrel divided and set slightly forward*
HACKLE: *Sparse brown saddle hackle, two or three turns should be sufficient*

This is one of Roderick Haig-Brown's patterns, one of the early true damp flies. Designed to fish the water's surface and not *in* the water, the sparse hackle serves its purpose well.

UMPQUA TAILWALKER

HOOK: *Low water or dry fly salmon hook; Mustad 90240, Tiemco 7989. Bend the front 1/3 of the hook up approximately 30 degrees*
TAIL: *Dark, stiff moose hair, optional*
BODY: *Dubbing or yarn in any of the following colors: Chartreuse, bright orange, caddis orange, golden-yellow or purple*
HACKLE: *Palmer saddle hackle of any corresponding color over the body*
THORAX: *Spun deer hair, either natural, black or purple. Clip flat on top and disc-shaped*
WING: *Dark stiff moose hair tied over the body and thorax, flared out. Leave about 1/4" of stub for the head and cement with five minute epoxy and flatten out and up*

Rick Abbott from Idleyld Park, Oregon developed this skater pattern on the North Umpqua. He showed me several prototypes of this fly before coming up with this final model. He ties the orange and yellow patterns for various caddis, salmonfly and stonefly hatches on the Umpqua. Purple, black and chartreuse are good basic steelhead colors. Rick also uses this bug during the hatches for big browns.

Dry Flies Plate 1

Autumn Liner (Birrell)

Beetle Bug (Helvie)

Bomber (Helvie)

Enterprise (Pettine)

Grizzly Wulff (Helvie)

MacIntosh (Helvie)

Royal Wulff (Rossano)

On Fire Liner (Birrell)

Rusty Popper (Birrell)

Dry Flies Plate 2

Seal Skater, Black (Helvie)

Seal Skater, Purple (Helvie)

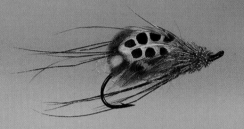

Soft Water Sedge (Birrell)

Soldier Palmer (Helvie)

Speed Skater, Grizzly/Brown (Rossano)

Speed Skater, Dark (Rossano)

Steelhead Bee (Helvie)

Umpqua Tailwalker (Abbott)

INDEX

BIBLIOGRAPHY

Bates, Joseph D., Jr., *The Art of the Atlantic Salmon Fly*, Boston, Massachusetts:
David R Godine, Publisher, Inc. 1987.

————. *Streamer Fly Tying and Fishing*, Harrisburg, Pennsylvania:
The Stackpole Company, 1950 and 1966.

Combs, Trey, *The Steelhead Trout*, Portland, Oregon:
Frank Amato Publications, Inc., second printing, 1988.

Combs, Trey, *Steelhead Fly Fishing and Flies*, Portland, Oregon:
Frank Amato Publications, Inc., 1976.

Combs, Trey, *Steelhead Fly Fishing*, New York, New York:
Lyons and Burford, 1991.

Dunham, Judith, *The Atlantic Salmon Fly, The Tiers and Their Art*, San Francisco, California:
Chronicle Books, 1991.

Hardy, John James, *Salmon Fishing*, London, England:
Country Life Ltd., 1907.

Frodin, Mikeal, *Classic Salmon Flies, History & Patterns*, Gothenburg, Sweden:
AB Nordbok, 1991.

Kelson, George M., *The Salmon Fly*, American reprint, Goshen, Connecticut:
The Anglers and Shooters Press, 1979.

Pryce-Tannatt, T. E., *How to Dress Salmon Flies*, London, England:
A&C Black, 1986 reprint.

Scott, Jock, *Greased Line Fishing For Salmon [and Steelhead]*, Portland, Oregon:
Frank Amato Publications, Inc., reprint, 1982.

Stewart, Dick & Allen Farrow, *Flies For Steelhead*, Intervale, New Hampshire:
Northland Press Inc., 1992.

Waltham, James, *Classic Salmon Flies*, The Francis Francis Collection, London, England:
A&C Black Publishers Ltd., 1983.

LEARN MORE ABOUT FLY FISHING AND FLY TYING WITH THESE BOOKS

If you are unable to find the books shown below at your local book store
or fly shop you can order direct from the publisher below.

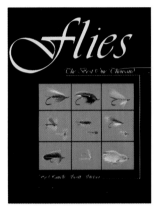

Flies: The Best One Thousand
Randy Stetzer
$24.95

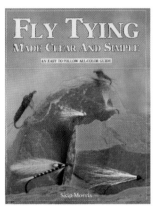

Fly Tying Made Clear and Simple
Skip Morris
$19.95 (HB: $29.95)

The Art of Tying the Dry Fly
Skip Morris
$29.95(HB:$39.95)

Curtis Creek Manifesto
Sheridan Anderson
$7.95

American Fly Tying Manual
Dave Hughes
$9.95

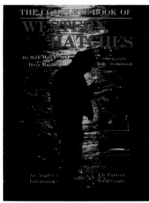

The Art and Science of Fly Fishing
Lenox Dick
$19.95

Western Hatches
Dave Hughes, Rick Hafele
$24.95

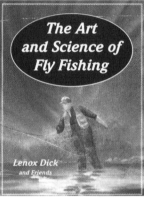

Lake Fishing with a Fly
Ron Cordes, Randall Kaufmann
$26.95

Advanced Fly Fishing for Steelhead
Deke Meyer
$29.95

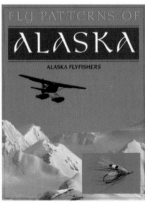

Fly Patterns of Alaska
Alaska Flyfishers
$19.95

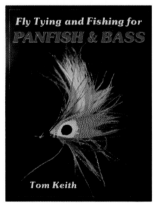

Fly Tying & Fishing for Panfish and Bass
Tom Keith
$19.95

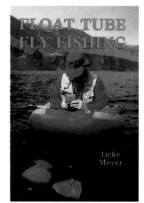

Float Tube Fly Fishing
Deke Meyer
$11.95

VISA, MASTERCARD or AMERICAN EXPRESS ORDERS CALL TOLL FREE: 1-800-541-9498
(9-5 Pacific Standard Time)

Or Send Check or money order to:

Frank Amato Publications
Box 82112
Portland, Oregon 97282

(Please add $3.00 for shipping and handling)